BETRAYED GENERATION

Shattered hopes and disillusion in post war Czechoslovakia.

Gerta Vrbová

First published MMX in Great Britain by
Zuza Books
www.zuzabooks.com

ISBN 978-1-907890-10-9

Printed in Great Britain by MPG, Biddles Ltd, Kings Lynn, UK.

To my daughter, Dr Helena Vrbová

ACKNOWLEDGEMENTS

My deep-felt thanks to my friends and colleagues in Czechoslovakia, Hungary, Poland, Denmark and England, who helped me to cope with my mistakes, and often took great risks to do so. This is particularly true of Dr. Andrzej Zbrożyna, without whose help I would never have been able to accomplish my escape from Czechoslovakia. I am grateful to Professor Olga Hudlická for her comments to the manuscript, her help with being more accurate about events we shared and the photographs, some of which are included in the book. I am grateful to Dr.Jenny Furey for her encouragement and for pointing out that the manuscript contains many mistakes. My thanks to my children Zuza, Caroline and Peter and their partners Andrew, Tim and Jane for their encouragement and affection while preparing the manuscript. I appreciate the patience of my grandchildren who often had to put up with discussions of my reminiscences, some of which must have been boring. I am indebted to Professor Rudolf Klein CBE, who corrected some of my English. The mistakes left are entirely my responsibility. My particular thanks to Zuza Vrbová without whose help and encouragement this book would not have been published.

Contents

Introduction

Fiction is history which might have taken place and history fiction which has taken place. (A.Gide, *The Vatican Cellars* p. 88).

The present narrative is a sequel to my autobiography *Trust and Deceit* that describes my experiences during the Second World War when, as a Jewish teenager, I managed to survive. In it, I relate how my life continued in communist Czechoslovakia and later in the West.

Starting a new life was much harder then I expected. My past experience and lack of a normal life between the years of 1939 and 1945 made me different from the rest of the people of my own age. Nevertheless, most people of our generation in Czechoslovakia had many things in common. After the horrific experiences of the Second World War we yearned to build a just society and lasting peace. The memories of the betrayal of our country in 1938 by our Western Allies—France and England—that culminated in the Munich Agreement, led young people of our generation to search for new solutions. The Soviet Union and Communist Party seemed to offer answers to our problems. In this book I describe how the search for a novel political solution, drove me and many others in Czechoslovakia to support the rise of the Communist Party to power. Thus I, like many others, embraced with great enthusiasm the communist ideology. Unfortunately, for our generation our hope that communism would lead to a more dignified society was short-lived and soon crushed by the unmistakable evidence of unfairness, inefficiency, lack of freedom and cruelty of the new totalitarian Communist Regime. The initial hope, enthusiasm and trust in the Communist Party and its leaders was followed by deep disenchantment with the system we had supported.

By giving an account of my life, first as a student, and then as a medical doctor and research scientist in communist Czechoslovakia, I have tried to illustrate, on a very personal level, what drove us to support the Communist Party and what life was like under communism for ordinary people. Retracing my life under communism from memories now, reveals that in spite of many restrictions and many disadvantages, the life of ordinary people was not entirely 'bad'. Although we had to endure many hardships, we lacked freedom of expression, we could not travel and had no freedom to pursue scientific and cultural activities unhindered, there were some aspects of society that gave some of its members, particularly women, more freedom than in the West.

Nevertheless glimpses of life in the West highlighted the fact that our lives under communism were impoverished. Finally, special circumstances in my personal life, when I was not allowed to marry the man I loved because he was an Englishman made me realize that I could no longer tolerate the restrictions that curtailed my freedom. In a carefully planned and dangerous enterprise I managed to escape with my two young daughters in 1958, first to Denmark and then to England, where I settled. In the West I experienced different prejudices and difficulties from those in communist Czechoslovakia, but the quality of life and opportunities we had were certainly better in the West.

Introduction

Since this narrative is a sequel to *Trust and Deceit* which descibes my experiences during the Second World War and these experiences had a profound influence on my actions described in the present book, I would like to include a brief summary of *Trust and Deceit.*

I was born in Trnava, a town in Western Slovakia close to Bratislava, the capital of Slovakia, into a middle class Jewish family. Until 1939, when I was 12 years old, I was not aware that I was any different from my non-Jewish neighbours. It therefore came as a shock, when my non-Jewish friends suddenly rejected me. At the same time the fascist Slovak government introduced a number of restrictions concerning the Jewish population, including the expulsion of all Jewish children from schools. Like the rest of Jewish children, Rudi my childhood friend and I were not allowed to attend school. I was 12 and Rudi 14 years old. We tried to continue our education by ourselves as best we could. Rudi was interested in chemistry and he converted a shed at the back of his mother's garden into a laboratory, where he conducted experiments. Sometimes I was allowed to witness how, as if by magic, Rudi could change the colours of various solutions, or filter papers or change the consistency of a substance by adding something else. These mysteries apparently had quite logical explanations and Rudi tried to teach me these principles. All went well, until one day by some mistake Rudi's laboratory exploded, and we could no longer watch the magical events. I introduced Rudi to my father, and my father suggested that Rudi could also teach me mathematics and physics. So I had my tutor, and I became very fond of him. Rudi, on the other hand, treated me as a child, far too young to be taken seriously, and that hurt a lot. In spite of all the restrictions and humiliations, we Jewish children managed to cope and survive. A dramatic change in our lives occurred in the spring of 1942 when the deportations to concentration camps started. The Slovak government made a deal with the German authorities to pay 500 deutsche marks for every Slovak Jew removed from Slovakia. Like everywhere else in Slovakia in Trnava too, most of the Jews older than 16 were taken to concentration camps.

My family had relatives in Hungary where the persecution of Jews had not yet been implemented and we escaped there. The border between Hungary and Slovakia was not impenetrable, and in the middle of a moonless night my parents and I walked across from Slovakia to Hungary. In Budapest we were able to purchase forged papers and with the help of our relatives managed to live under assumed identities. I had to learn all the details of my new persona, and above all to speak Hungarian, a language I was not familiar with. Nevertheless, our escape to Hungary meant my parents and I were lucky to avoid the first wave of deportations from Slovakia.

In the spring of 1944 the political situation in Hungary changed and the Hungarians assisted the Germans in rounding up the Jews and sending them to concentration camps. My father was detained and imprisoned by the Hungarian police and my mother and I had to move from our lodgings to escape deportation. We had nowhere to go and since in Slovakia the round up of Jews was now considered complete we returned to Slovakia, taking the same route across the Hungarian-Slovak border we had taken two years previously, in the opposite direction.

In Bratislava my mother and I took on another assumed identity and we lived in Bratislava during the spring and summer of 1944. While in Bratislava I met my childhood friend Rudi again. He was one of the very few people who escaped from the death camp Auschwitz and was determined to tell the world about the atrocities and crimes committed there. He was aware that the Germans were planning to eliminate the Hungarian Jews and wanted to warn them about these preparations. He and his friend Freddie Wetzler, who also escaped from Auschwitz, wrote an extensive report, now known as *The Auschwitz Protocols* or the *Vrba-Wetzler Report*. It was from Rudi that I learned about what was happening in Auschwitz and other death camps, and this information would influence a later decision which saved my life.

In the autumn of 1944 there was a Partisan uprising in Slovakia. Rudi joined the Partisans but I stayed in Bratislava when the Germans marched into Slovakia and occupied it. Soon after this the remaining Jews were again rounded up, and in spite of our assumed identity my mother and I were taken by the Gestapo and identified as Jews. It was at the Gestapo headquarters that I had to make the most difficult decision: should I escape or stay with my mother, who refused to escape, or, leave her and survive? Had I not known from Rudi what to expect if I did not escape, I probably would have stayed with my mother, but the knowledge about the certain and humiliating death that awaited us if we were to be taken to concentration camp made me decide to escape. After my escape from the Gestapo I was helped by Slovak friends to gain enough time to organize my return to Hungary, again crossing the Slovak-Hungarian border illegally.

I was hoping to find my father, but I never succeeded. By now it was the end of November 1944, and the Russian Army was just outside Budapest. This did not stop the Germans and the Hungarians who collaborated with the Germans from trying to destroy what was left of the Jewish population in Hungary. Now alone in Budapest I felt a strong urge to prevent this. I acquired another false identity and joined a group of young Jews, who tried to help other Jews by supplying them with forged papers and finding them places to hide. I was involved in distributing these documents to Jews in the Ghetto, who then could escape the Ghetto. On the 15th of January 1945 I was liberated by the Russian Army. I stayed in Hungary until the end of the war and in May 1945 returned to Trnava to start a new life.

Dedication to Helena

My daughter Helena Vrbová, London 1972.

In 1982, on the 9th of May a dark cloud carried the sun away, for on that day you, my firstborn daughter Helena died and left us for ever. I could visualize the beach house near Madang in Papua New Guinea, where you went to die. The unreal beauty of the spot could have been paradise, and yet when I heard that it was there that you died, it turned into the most sinister dark place on earth.

Taking a job in far away Papua New Guinea was but one of the manifestations of your intense desire to help people. You went there to fight malaria, and stayed for three years. You coped with your loneliness and had the strength to offer medical care to villagers that had never been cared for, and worked hard for the people there. You achieved so much and I cannot understand the despair that has driven you to opt out from life. I remember I felt a sense of unreality, when I visited you in Madang. The beauty of the place, all the alien plants, animals and smells made me feel that I was already on a different plane between being alive and dead, maybe this was already paradise and death is not so far away. The loneliness, and isolation from everything familiar must have engulfed you and in a moment of despair perhaps you forgot how much we loved you, and instead of coming back home to us, as you were supposed to, you departed, just before your 30th birthday on that dreadful journey, from where there is no return.

I am now 84 years old, and you left me for good 28 years ago. The pain of losing you does not go away. I keep wondering what I could have done to prevent your death. Maybe when you were old enough to understand, I should have explained to you how important you were for me and your father as well as the family. It was your birth and later your person that gave me the strength to live after the war. I was the only Holocaust survivor of our close family. Although your father Rudi, and I were married we were terribly lonely, and bruised by our experience during the Holocaust. Perhaps at the time we didn't comprehend, at all, how 'damaged' we both were, and it is only with time that I can see how it must have affected us all. It was you and your birth that helped me to live and do something useful with my life. I remember feeling you growing inside me and the exquisite pleasure of knowing that a new life is being created. Just a few years ago, Rudi and I had both been destined to die in the Holocaust, and now together we have created a new life, that was you Helena. I have never felt as content, at ease with myself and the world as when we were together and shared the same body.

When it was time for you to leave me you did it so gently. One morning at the end of May 1952 you were complete and ready to leave me. I went to hospital on my own. Rudi had to go and pick up a fridge for our small flat, and I took the tram to go to hospital. I arrived at the hospital and announced to the porter that I had started labour. The labour pains were now every five minutes and they were quite intense. The porter looked at me and said, 'You don't look as though you are in labour. You are too slim to be nine months pregnant. In addition, when women come to deliver a baby they don't come alone, and they bring a suitcase and a cushion and not just a briefcase like you. I think you had better go home.' I asked him to call Dr. Brodski who was my obstetrician and friend. Dr. Brodski came to see me immediately, and admitted me to the labour ward. He examined me and said,'you are right, you are in labour, your cervix is dilated and the baby should be delivered within the next two hours.' Soon after this, Helena, you were born and it hardly hurt at all. A cheerful midwife wrapped you in a shawl and brought you to me. She smiled and said: 'you have a beautiful baby.' You had a lot of dark hair a smooth dark face, a small nose, and when you opened your huge eyes and looked around, the whole world seemed different. To me you seemed to be the most exquisite human being on earth. Rudi came to see us later. He gave me a hug and kiss, and then took you into his arms and said to me, 'Gerti, if someone had told me in Auschwitz that in 10 years time I will be a father to such an exquisite baby I would not have believed it. Yet here she is, our daughter.' I asked Rudi, 'What should we call her?' 'Let's call her Helena after my mother, and because she certainly will be every bit as beautiful as Helen of Troy.' Rudi was always concerned with beauty. He was much too interested in appearances. I saw the inner beauty of your person in those huge baby eyes of yours, but Rudi saw the physical beauty you would acquire when you grew into a woman. Still you were named Helena, and the name suited you. A few days later we took you to our small apartment in Dejvice. At the time it was quite a luxury to have a two-room apartment, with a bathroom and a kitchenette. One room was used as a sitting- dining room, the other room was our bedroom. We had already bought a baby cot and that was in the bedroom, squeezed under the window. We had a baby bath for you, and we managed to obtain a plank of wood to put on the bath where we could change your nappies, and place the baby bath when you had a bath. We were so proud of all these preparations we had made for your arrival. When you arrived and entered our life I had completed my medical studies and Rudi had his degree in chemical engineering in Prague.

Before you entered our lives my best friends, together with Rudi and myself, had moved from Bratislava to Prague, and tried to start a new life to escape the shadow cast over us by the Holocaust. I wish I had given you some glimpses of our attempts to live and shared with you our past, but I didn't want to burden you with those memories of difficult times. So now, too late for you, I am writing about our lives for others to understand the difficult times we survivors of the Holocaust had, after the war had ended.

Chapter 1

Returning To Slovakia: May—September 1945

The entrance to my school in Trnava.

I returned from Budapest to my home town Trnava in May 1945, hoping that my parents had survived the Holocaust and would come back home. The train pulled into the railway station, stopped, and I left the train, carrying my small suitcase which contained my modest possessions, and headed off towards our house on the main square. At first glance little had changed in Trnava since I left more than three years ago in April 1942, yet I felt a stranger in my home town. As I walked towards our house, which I knew was now occupied by the family who had taken over my parent's shop and appropriated all our possessions, the memory of the betrayal by my former friend Marushka suddenly hit me and opened wounds I thought had healed.

On a lovely summer day in 1939 Marushka and I had gone for a bicycle trip to visit my uncle Karol who lived in a nearby village. We stopped to rest in the shade of a tree where Marushka told me that she would no longer be able to meet me because I was Jewish. She had been told by her parents that her friendship with me may jeopardize their chances to become owners of our house when, as Jews, we will have to leave Trnava to be 'resettled' somewhere else.

Thus, with these memories I was in a rather sombre mood when I reached our house. I stood outside the gate and looked at the solid building that was our family home. I remembered how hard my parents worked to have it built. For years my mother got up at six each morning and helped as a cashier in the butcher's shop, owned by our family. In winter these early mornings were bitterly cold and although she wore gloves that she herself knitted, with the fingertips exposed so she could handle the money, she could not avoid getting frostbite on her fingers. At ten o'clock she took the train to Bratislava where she ran her own business. When finally she returned home in the evening she always had time for me and the family.

I opened the wooden gate and entered the courtyard which I remembered housed many beautiful plants when we lived in the house, but there were none there now. As a child the courtyard was a place where I played out many of my fantasies: with my grandmother Jeanette's help, I wrote and organized plays which my friends and I performed in front of an audience of our parents and their friends.

Chapter 1

Me at the age of 6 in the courtyard of our house.

Here I learned to ride a bicycle, sat on a stool in the sun and dreamed about the future. Now I stood here alone in a place that had become barren, and considered my own present situation. I went outside and headed towards the butcher's shop that used to be my father's.

I knew I had to talk to Mr. Šimončič, the man who threw our family out of our home. The entrance to what used to be our shop was wide open and I found Mr. Šimončič in the almost empty shop sitting behind the counter. I noticed that he had become quite fat, and looked uglier than I remembered. The shop which used to be neat and tidy was now dirty and empty. When I entered the shop and Mr. Šimončič saw me he exclaimed with horror: 'You are still alive.' This statement of course did not need an answer. Nevertheless, I was taken by surprise, for I thought that he would be aware of the fact that the war was over, and that Slovakia had become part of the new Czechoslovak Republic which had come into being in April 1945. The new Czechoslovak democratic government was a coalition of three parties. The Slovak Popular Party was excluded, since during the war, it collaborated with the Nazis. Many of the leaders of the deposed fascist Slovak government were in prison and waiting to be tried for war crimes. In view of this political situation I expected Mr. Šimončič to be a little more helpful or perhaps even apologetic to me, but I was mistaken for when I asked him politely whether I could have just one room in our house which he and his family now occupied, he was quite dismayed and said: 'You cannot stay here, we have nowhere else to go and we need the whole house. You will have to find accommodation elsewhere. You can't just turn up and expect us to move out.' He refused to let me into the house, and I knew that there was no point in arguing with Mr. Šimončič who still didn't understand that the fascist lawlessness was now finished and that he would have to return the stolen property. I had nowhere else to go, and felt that it was my right to live in my house, and therefore I turned to the Russian authorities that were, at the time, in charge of administering accommodation in Trnava. (When the Russian army liberated Slovakia it took temporary charge of administering the occupied territories even before the official end of the war, and before the new Czechoslovak government had established a new administration). Thus to try to sort out my accommodation I went to the Russian authorities to ask for help.

The offices of the Russians were housed in the town hall and I found them easily. There was a sign marked ACCOMMODATION and I followed it. In a large office a smartly dressed Russian officer sat behind a desk and asked what my problem was. I explained that I had survived the Holocaust, and now had returned home after three years and wanted to wait for my parents, who had not yet returned from concentration camp. I needed accommodation and wanted to stay in the house that my parents owned, but have been denied any room in the house by the present occupier of the house. The Russian officer who listened to my account, offered to sort out my problem. He smiled at me and introduced himself: 'I am Sergej, and what shall I call you?' I told him to call me Gerta, and we set off immediately to our house. From the town hall in the main street we walked along the small narrow cobbled street that led to our house. It was a strange feeling walking along these streets again, which felt both familiar and alien now. We knocked at the gate and Mr. Šimončič let us in. The Russian officer explained to Mr. Šimončič that he had to provide me with accommodation. Then he turned to me and asked me which room I wanted. At first I thought I would like to have my old room back. I ran up the stairs and headed towards the room that used to be mine, but when I opened the door, my heart stopped for a minute, for now it was Šimončič's daughter Marushka's room, and there was nothing in it that reminded me of my old room. I didn't recognize it at all and felt that it would be too painful to move into this room. Instead, I asked for the room that used to be my parent's bedroom. It was a good sized room with attractive rosewood furniture, two beds in the centre, two bedside cabinets, a bookshelf and two wardrobes facing the window. The window overlooked the main square and the bright curtains allowed a lot of light to enter the room. In front of each bed the pale parquet floor was covered by a Persian rug. I also wanted the room to be ready for my parents when they returned home. 'That is fine,' said Sergej, and took out a piece of paper and a pen, summoned Mr. Šimončič and told him to immediately vacate the room I had chosen and give me the keys to the house and my room. The Russian officer handed Mr. Šimončič a signed order to confirm that I was entitled to live in the house. After completing this transaction, Sergej whom I now considered to be a friend, left and told me that if I had any problems I should contact him. But there were no problems, and since I had hardly any possessions, it was easy for me to move in.

I avoided seeing the members of the family who still lived in the house and spent most of my time looking at lists of returning and missing people, which were displayed in the office of the Jewish community centre, and also in an office run by the Red Cross. Day after day I went there and read hundreds of names, but the names of my parents did not appear on any of the lists. Sometimes I met people who had returned from various camps. They looked emaciated, indifferent and very sad. I asked everyone whether they knew anything about my parents, but there was never any news. As the days passed my hopes of finding my parents dwindled, and my desperation deepened.

In addition to the lack of success in finding any news about my parents I found myself in a place, my home town, that was both familiar and alien to me. As I walked the streets and visited places I used to know, everything was the same and yet different from what I remembered. The delicatessen shop in the main street, where I often went shopping and where I knew and liked the owners of the shop who usually served me, was still there, but the people in the shop were no longer the original Jewish owners and I didn't know them. Places where my friends and I used to meet and walk seemed unfamiliar. The memory of my friends with whom I used to walk along the streets in Trnava before I left home was with me and the knowledge that most of them were slaughtered in the camps and would never return, made my stay in Trnava a misery. My gloomy mood was not helped by new experiences in Trnava. It was still term time, and I went to the gate of the school that I used to attend till 1939. It was at this very gate where in September 1939 my Jewish friends and I were told that we were not allowed to enter the school, and where my schoolmates shouted at us 'Jews out'. I don't know what I expected, but perhaps I was still naïve enough to hope that if some of my former school mates recognized me, they would be pleased to see me and apologize for their behaviour. So I stood outside the gate waiting till the lessons finished and then watched my former schoolmates leaving the school. I was surprised that in spite of the change in their appearance during the six years I had been away, I could recognize some of them. I thought that they too would recognize me, but they went past me as though I didn't exist. Not one them acknowledged my presence, yet alone stopped to talk to me or apologize.

To restore my faith in humanity, I went to visit my father's friend Mr. Pavelka who had always been helpful to our family. My parents had given him some of our possessions before we left our home, to keep for us and return them on our return to Trnava. He and his family received me with open arms and were pleased to see me and Mr. Pavelka was anxious to know what had happened to my parents, but I had no news for him. In spite of the warm welcome I felt that my visit caused embarrassment, and that the family was ashamed for the behaviour of their fellow Slovak citizens. They offered to return to me all our things they had kept for us, but I only took one towel as a souvenir. I had nowhere to take the rest, the fur coats, carpets, and jewellery. I didn't visit them again. How could I care about furs, jewellery, and other posessions when my family might be dead? Sergej came occasionally to see me and helped me with my search, but when after three weeks nothing happened I knew that to continue with the search as my sole occupation would destroy me and that I needed to think ahead.

And then at last, after all these depressing and miserable days, when I had to come to terms with the fact that my home town had been irretrievably lost for me things started to improve. I found out that my friend Inge and her mother had survived the war and were back in Trnava in their old flat. Suddenly, a glimmer of hope started to penetrate the darkness I seemed to have experienced since my arrival 'home'. The hope was inspired by having a friend with whom I had so much in common.

Just being in their flat brought back torrents of memories. I remembered that just before the war started I was chosen to read some Slovak poetry at the school assembly, and I selected some very patriotic Slovak poems. Inge and I were sitting on the same settee we sat on now and Inge, who was much more realistic than I, warned me that it was not appropriate for me to read such patriotic poetry for I could not be accepted as a Slovak patriot. At the time I refused to understand what she meant, but now I knew that even then, before the war, as a Jew, I was not accepted as a Slovak. It was a real gift to have a friend with whom I had so much in common, with whom I had shared my childhood. Being with Inge, helped me to pull myself together and overcome the despair I felt when I started to realize that my parents might never return.

Chapter 1

When I first saw Inge after the war I was surprised how thin and pale she was. Her large blue eyes set in her haggard face seemed even bigger then I remembered. But when she explained that she was hidden in a loft of a peasant family outside Trnava for four months and never went out, I understood why she was so pale. That was how she avoided being deported, and being hidden saved her life. Her mother's employer, a member of the local Council and a supporter of the fascist government was very fond of her mother and when he intercepted the order for her and Inge's deportation he made arrangements to find a hiding place for them. Thus, although a fascist, this man saved my friend and her mother from an almost certain death.

Inge and I met quite frequently, and our renewed friendship continued to give me strength to cope with the loneliness I felt after my daily hopeless search for my parents. We went for long walks and Inge even more then I, enjoyed the freedom of being able to be outside. It was spring and as we walked in the park we observed with pleasure the awakening of the trees, bushes and meadows from their winter sleep, and the display of the different shades of the tender light green colours.

There was a particular bench that captured the sun most of the day that we liked to sit on and talk. During one of our walks through the park we sat down on 'our bench' and talked about our future and our dream to go and study at University. Inge told me that she was fascinated by physics and chemistry, because those disciplines she thought, might explain the secrets of the world surrounding us and that she wanted to study chemistry. At this stage we had no idea how we would be able to get access to University since we missed so much of our secondary school education and did not have the necessary qualifications for University studies. Neither of us were allowed to attend secondary school after 1939. Now six years later, in 1945, we tried to figure out how to catch up on all the learning and knowledge we had missed, for without this we could not continue our education. Thus unless we could catch up on our education, attending University would remain a dream.

Then suddenly, something happened that made it possible for the dream to turn to reality. One day Inge came to see me and without even saying 'Hello', reported: 'My mother just had the news that the Education Department of the Czechoslovak Republic has started to organize some courses for young people who were unable to attend school during the war, such as the two of us. Apparently in these courses the whole syllabus of secondary school education will be taught. If we pass the final exams we will be able to go to University.' With the help of Inge's mother and some searching we found out that such a course was being organized in Bratislava.

Inge and I were ecstatic and immediately set off for Bratislava to find out about these courses. We located the school where they were to be held, and enrolled straight away. The course was due to start in the middle of June, and it was the end of May now, so we didn't have time to waste. We had much work to do to prepare for attending the course. We needed accommodation and I needed some money for living expenses. Inge and I found a small room we could share in the outskirts of Bratislava where we had to pay little rent. But even this expense was too much for me for I had no money at all, and had only about two weeks to earn enough to enable me to pay for my living expenses while attending the course.

Securing my finances.

Meanwhile some members of my extended family had returned from concentration camps or had come out of hiding, and I hoped they would help with advice about my future. But they were trying to put their own lives together and had little time for me. I tried to discuss my plans to study and go to University with them, but they were not very supportive of my intentions to study, and thought I should just try to get some kind of job. So yet again I was left to my own resources to solve my problems, which in the first instance were financial. Somehow I managed to do so, by following the advice from my cousin's boyfriend Alfred, who was a very astute business man. Originally from Vienna he survived the war as a refugee in Budapest, where my parents helped him to hide. Due to his very Jewish appearance he could not move freely and my parents and I looked after him. Now Alfred tried to be helpful and gave me some useful advice.

Alfred's skills included making money on the black market and I wanted to learn from him how to do it. When I asked him what I should do, he gave me this advice: 'You buy something, and sell it for more money.' I was at a loss, wondering what I should buy, when suddenly it occurred to me that there were many shops where the illegal owners who had appropriated the shops from their previous Jewish owners wanted to sell various items rather fast, so as to avoid returning them to the previous owners of the shops, if they returned from concentration camps, or if the shops were nationalized by the state. Selling their stock, albeit cheaply would still give them some financial advantage. So I went round shops that were selling materials for dresses or coats, for I was quite adept at assessing the quality of such fabrics and bought some at rather favourable prices. In Bratislava many enterprising tailors and dressmakers were setting up small dressmaking workshops and needed a selection of materials. To these I could sell the materials I bought at a good price and make some profit. These transactions usually took place in the Carlton coffee bar, a great centre for various illegal activities such as currency exchange. I got to know quite a few serious 'blackmarketeers' who made a fortune during these few post war months. But I was quite modest, I worked out how much money I needed to start me off, and once I earned enough I stopped working. In fact I had to stop, for our course was about to begin and I did not have time to travel around and buy and sell goods. Also I was getting bored with this activity.

Attending school.

Among several others who attended the course was Rudi, my childhood friend who now lived in Bratislava with his mother Ilonka. Rudi was a real hero, for he was one of the only five people who had escaped from Auschwitz. I had tremendous admiration for him. Inge and I also befriended a girl called Eva. She survived the war as a hidden child in Budapest and after the war returned with her mother and sister to their home in Nitra in Slovakia. She also came to Bratislava to attend the same course as Inge, Rudi and I. Eva was the same age as Inge and I. She was a small and plump girl, with short black curls framing her face. Like Inge and I, she too used all her energy trying to keep up with the rather demanding course work. She had a great advantage over most of us, having an extraordinarily good memory. Once she heard or saw something she always remembered it. She was also very capable at finding out where we could get cheap tasty food and how to find bargains for things we needed, such as school books, pens and pencils. She was very generous and always shared her discoveries with us. The course ran for three months and covered the syllabus taught over a period of six years in normal secondary schools (*gymnasiums*). The course started at eight in the morning and our days were crammed with lectures, practicals and tutorials. When the lessons finished, usually around six in the evening, Inge and I returned to our small rented room, had a short break and then continued to study. We hardly slept at all, but our desire to pass the exams at the end of the three months so that we could start University in September, was so strong that it suppressed our need for sleep.

Finally the day came when the results of our examinations were to be announced. Inge and I took the tram to the school building and went with all the other pupils to the main assembly hall. Everyone was very apprehensive, for so much depended on whether or not we passed our exams. I was not sure whether I had passed all exams. I was particularly concerned about my geography exam, for on the day of the final geography exam I had put on new shoes that hurt my feet, and during the oral exam when I was standing in front of the map and was supposed to point out the various places I wrote about in my essay, I could not think clearly. My feet ached terribly, and that was all I could think of. But I knew that in all other subjects, particularly science, I had done well, so when the Head Teacher went to the front of the class with a piece of paper in his hand to read out the names of those who passed, I was not unduly worried. The tension in the room was palpable, for now the future of all the 25 young people from our course was to be revealed. The Head Teacher read out the names of those who had passed. There were only five of us who had passed all the exams and Eva, Inge, Rudi and I were among them. We were ecstatic with joy. We were told to pick up our certificates of matriculation that entitled us to enter University, later in the afternoon.

That evening, to celebrate our success, Rudi's mother Ilonka, invited Inge, Eva and me for dinner. With all the food shortages we expected a modest meal, perhaps with a bottle of wine to accompany the food. To our great surprise, a most sumptuous meal was served. Roast duck stuffed with plums, served with red cabbage and roast potatoes. As a dessert Rudi's mother produced a most delicious chocolate cake, topped with whipped cream. It was incomprehensible to us how Rudi's mother, Ilonka, managed to assemble the ingredients for this feast, but we were delighted to have such a wonderful treat. The only person who looked festive and smart at that dinner party was Ilonka. She had had her hair done at a hairdresser, was dressed in a smart navy suit, and her voluminous breasts presided over the dinner table with obvious authority. Perhaps I should not have been surprised that she had managed to assemble such a feast in those meagre times, for she was incredibly inventive and skillful in acquiring rare commodities. During the war she was taken to Terezín concentration camp, managed to convince the Nazi guards that she was an excellent seamstress and could provide high quality ladies underwear for the German ladies. She was given facilities to open a small workshop, where she helped others to survive by employing them as helpers, and her workshop provided fancy lingerie for the wives and daughters of the Nazi leadership. Even in Terezín she was always able to manage and also help others.

After our meal we had real Turkish-style coffee, served in small delicate porcelain cups. We were all relaxed and in a happy mood. Rudi's mother sat majestically at the head of the table, her blue eyes smiling with pleasure that her guests enjoyed the meal. Then she became serious, and asked: 'What will you do now?' We were taken aback by this turn of the mood to serious discussions. 'We would like to go to Prague and study there,' said Rudi. His mother didn't say anything, but I noticed that she was saddened by this news. She would, of course have preferred for her son, who had so miraculously survived the war, to be near her. So we tried to explain how we felt, and why we wanted to leave Slovakia. 'Look Ilonka Néni ,' I tried to answer the question that hung in the air, but no one asked, 'all of us had such terrible experiences here in Slovakia and so little sympathy from our Slovak neighbours we would rather start a new life somewhere else. Nobody helped us, or showed sympathy when we were thrown out of our houses and worse, deported to the death camps. And when we returned after most awful experiences, most people were disappointed that we were still alive. We don't want to go abroad, Czechoslovakia is our home, but Prague is a place where we could start life unburdened by sad memories. Also it is a bigger and more cosmopolitan city than Bratislava, and it is near enough for us to visit you and for you to come and see us.' She seemed to understand, at least we thought so. Or maybe she just didn't want to spoil our happy mood. This was a very special evening, full of warmth and understanding, some reminder of home.

After this we started our preparation for our departure to Prague.

Final farewell to Trnava.

For the last time I went back to Trnava and checked, once more, whether anyone had heard anything about my parents. But there was no news. I had to resign myself and accept the sad reality that my parents would not return. There was another matter I had to attend to before leaving for Prague. It concerned my house. It was returned to me, but without my parents around and me going away, I did not want the house. I was at a loss what to do with it, so when my neighbour who had always been good to us, asked me to sell it to him I was very pleased. But he had no money, so I agreed to sell him the house in exchange for a Leica camera, a typewriter and a gold watch. There was just one condition: 'Please make sure that the Šimončič family will have to leave the house.' He promised that he would get them out of our house. After I tended to these matters I was ready to move on.

The journey to Prague.

The 18th September 1945 was a mild autumn evening in Bratislava. Our first free autumn after all those years of war, danger and horror. Inge, Rudi, Eva and I were waiting for the train for Prague and standing on a crowded platform in Bratislava's main railway station. We were ready to start our University education. Inge and Rudi wanted to study chemical engineering and Eva and I medicine. During the three summer months we had time for nothing else except hard work and not much time was left to think about our future. I remember some of our rare discussions. One afternoon when the sun was out and we really needed a break, Inge and I went for a walk along the embankment of the Danube and sat down on a bench. I asked Inge: 'Do you know what you want to study?' She had no reservation and replied: 'Chemistry, and what about you Gerti?' My decision was not that straight forward, in fact I was very ambiguous about my future. 'I really would like to be a film director, but I am not sure whether I have enough talent, and whether I could make a living as a film director. So maybe I will study medicine.' In the end, no matter what subject we chose, all four of us wanted to study in Prague and not here in Bratislava. So there we were in the railway station in Bratislava, waiting for the overnight train to Prague. There was just one train a day running between Bratislava and Prague, and this was not enough to cope with all those who wanted to travel. There were more passengers than room on the train.

Even before we could see the train we could hear the noise and smell the smoke. It was puffing and huffing and releasing lots of smoke, for its engine was fuelled with bad quality coal. The whole platform was engulfed in smoke and steam, but the crowds of people waiting for the train were oblivious to the smell and vapours that stung the eyes and made it hard to breathe. There were so many people it was impossible to move, for as usual when a train was expected, the platform was filled with too many passengers and it was clear that not all of them will be able to board the train. We worked out a plan how to get on the train. Rudi and Inge would jump on the train as soon as it slowed down, even before it stopped. Eva and I would look after the luggage and hand the luggage to Rudi and Inge through the window when the train stopped, and then climb through the window into the compartment secured by Inge and Rudi. 'Well here we go,' we said as we pushed Inge and

Rudi through the door of the still moving train. Crowds of people were pushing us in all directions as Eva and I looked for a window to open to push the luggage through the window and climb in. After a while, Rudi's head appeared out of one of the windows and we handed him our luggage, and then were ready to climb in ourselves. Eva clasped Rudi's hand and I lifted her up so she could reach the window. Eva was on the train but I was on the platform with no one to help me. As the train started to move I jumped holding up my hands. Rudi leaned out of the window, got hold of one hand and the sleeve of my jacket of the other arm and tried to lift me into the carriage through the window. But the window was very high and without help on the platform I could not climb in. The train started to depart and moved slowly along the platform and I was still outside. Rudi pulled hard on my jacket sleeve to lift me through the window. It was my best jacket and one I specially wanted to have with me to make a good impression. Finally with all his help and strength I managed to haul myself up, but at the last minute, when I was almost in the carriage, the sleeve of my jacket ripped. Still, I was on the train, and I would just have to mend my jacket later. We had one seat between the four of us and decided to take it in turns. Those of us who were standing were kept upright by the other passengers, for the train was so crowded and there was no danger of toppling over. Also, we were so tired that it didn't matter whether we stood up, or sat down; we managed to sleep in either position. Finally after eight hours we arrived in Prague's main station, Wilsonovo Nádraží. The station was named after the American President Woodruff Wilson, who helped to bring about the existence of the new Republic of Czechoslovakia after the First World War. Stiff from the journey our clothes creased, aching all over we arrived in Prague.

Chapter 2
Starting Off In Prague

My boyfriend Rudi and I, in Prague 1947.

So it was early on a Monday morning that Rudi, Eva, Inge and I found ourselves admiring the *Art Nouveau* architecture of Prague's main station Wilsonovo Nádraží. We were too tired to appreciate properly the magnificent entrance hall but we managed to find the left luggage department and deposited our luggage there. In our crumpled and tattered clothes we set out to make arrangements for our studies in Prague. Our first task was to find the place where students enrolled for their courses. We were given the address of the office where to enrol by our teacher in Bratislava, but none of us had ever been to Prague, and we did not have a map of Prague so we asked people on the street to direct us to Spálená Ulice and followed their directions. It was not very far to walk and we were quite pleased to stretch our legs. Finally after some mistakes and wondering around we found the right street and building where the registration office was, where students were to enrol for their respective courses.

While still in Bratislava we were warned that because we came from Slovakia and there was a Slovak university in Bratislava, we might not be accepted to study in Prague. We were advised that if asked why we wish to study in Prague, rather then Bratislava, we should claim that we chose Prague, because we had family there and the family might give us some financial support. Briefly, when asked why we wanted to study in Prague we were advised to answer: 'for economic reasons'.

During six years of German occupation all Czech Universities were closed. It was therefore not surprising that the registration office was full of young people, eager to start studying. Most of the students were older than us, some of them as old as 25, for after six years of waiting they were at last allowed to enter University. In spite of the large crowds of young people fillling the registration office everything was well organized. There were several desks manned by young people and the subject for which one could enrol at a particular desk was clearly marked on a cardboard poster. Eva and I joined a long queue in front of a desk marked MEDICINE and waited for our turn. We were apprehensive and worried about possible difficulties, but when we reached the desk, a young woman smiled at us and asked: 'You want to study Medicine? Please hand me the certificate showing that you have finished secondary school, and passed the right exams.' We had our papers ready, and in no time we got a document confirming that we were enrolled to study medicine at the Charles University. We were told: 'The lectures start in ten days' time, and I hope you enjoy the course.' And that was it, nobody asked us any questions, and for us the whole atmosphere in the room seemed suddenly to be filled with joy and excitement. We met Rudi and Inge and they too had no difficulty registering to study chemical engineering.

Our next task was to find accommodation. Housing for students was available at a number of colleges, and it was allotted to those who had already enrolled to study a particular subject. Eva and I were now medical students and Inge and Rudi had enrolled to study chemistry, so all of us were 'active' students. Accommodation was allotted separately to women and men. Inge, Eva and I were sent to a different counter from Rudi. Behind the counter was a young, very serious man who examined our document confirming our 'student status' and then said: 'There is no accommodation for you for tonight, but tomorrow you can move into a room in a college in 6, Hradební Ulice (Hradební Street).' He took out a map of Prague and pointed out where Hradební Ulice was. We were excited, for it was very near the old Town Square, in the city centre. The next announcement however was a bit of a blow:

'However, there is no furniture in the place and you will have to get the furniture yourselves from a furniture depot.' We were given the address of the depot and some vouchers to obtain three beds and a wardrobe. Rudi was luckier, for as from the next day he was offered accommodation in a furnished room in a college for men, close to the Chemistry Department in Dejvice, where he would study, about two miles from the centre of the town.

But tonight we had nowhere to go and too little money to go to a decent hotel. Our next task therefore was to find rooms in a place where we could afford to stay for one night. First we went to the railway station to pick up our luggage. We all had backpacks, and Eva's was the most spectacular. It was even shabbier than ours and she had a huge umbrella sticking out from her green backpack. All four of us in our crumpled clothes, looked exactly like what we were: inexperienced newcomers from the country who could easily be taken for a ride. And we were.

Tired and worried, we waited at a tram stop outside the station. We got on the first tram that came along and asked the conductor whether he knew of a cheap hotel where we could stay the night. He took a good look at us and told us that there is a place in Karlín (a suburb of Prague) where we could stay. He kept a straight face and promised that he would tell us where to get off the tram. We were really pleased, for we felt completely exhausted and the prospect of a bed after our uncomfortable journey and tiring day was irresistible. After several stops, the conductor told us to get off the tram and pointed out the hotel he thought would be suitable. It was called *Hotel Nitra*, and it indeed, looked cheap. The four of us entered the hotel lobby. There was a threadbare carpet and a sign that said: RECEPTION. Behind a simple wooden counter stood a shabby, skinny man, and on the wall behind him were hooks with the keys to the rooms. We asked for two rooms, one for Rudi and one for us, the three girls. Although we got some strange looks from the receptionist, we didn't notice anything unusual about the place and gratefully took the keys to our rooms. Our room had a single bed and a sofa. We decided that Inge and I will sleep in the bed and Eva on the sofa. There was a wash basin in the room with taps for hot and cold water. Inge wanted to look her best the next day, so she washed her hair and used newspaper strips, instead of curlers, to perfect her hairstyle. Eva and I just put on our old-fashioned flanelette white nightdresses and went straight to sleep.

In the middle of the night we were woken up from our deep sleep by a knock on the door. Eva on the sofa was closest to the door, so she opened it. Two policemen stood in the door and stared at us. When they came in and took in the scene with me and Inge sleeping in a single bed and Eva on the sofa, our shabby backpacks by the window, they looked puzzled, and one of them asked: 'Why are you here?' Suddenly Inge woke up, sat up in the bed with the crumpled newspaper curlers in her hair, half asleep and confused, blurted out the answer she was told to give when registering to study: 'For economic reasons.' Both the policemen started to laugh uncontrollably. Then they asked us whether we had any idea what kind of a hotel this was. We really didn't understand the question. 'It is just a cheap hotel.' Eva replied. Finally one of the policemen explained that this was a 'Hodinový'—meaning hourly—hotel, where prostitutes brought their clients for an hour or so to have sex. None of us had ever heard of a place like that, and we were surprised that such a place existed. The policemen thought that we had provided them with enough amusement for one night and just told us to go back to sleep and move out in the morning. This we intended to do anyway. So this was where we spent our first night in Prague.Next morning we split up, Rudi had a furnished room in a men's college in Dejvice near the technical high school, and did not need any furniture. Eva, Inge and I went to Hradební Ulice to inspect our room. We started off from the old Town Square (Staroměstkě Náměstí) and walked through the old town along Dlouhá Ulice (Long Street) to reach our destination, Hradební Ulice.

We couldn't help but be enchanted by the city. In spite of the greyness and shabbiness of the buildings, this old part of the city was bewitching by its beauty. The history of Prague was visible everywhere and the Gothic and Renaissance buildings blended perfectly into the rather modest Czech Baroque. When we reached the college we met the concierge who showed us to our room. It was a large room on the ground floor. As expected the room was empty, not only of people but also of furniture. There were communal bathrooms at the end of our corridor and a communal kitchen—equipped with several cookers, kettles, pots, pans and crockery. To get our furniture we had to go to a depot in Žižkov, a suburb of Prague, situated about four kilometres from the old town and our accommodation. We took the tram and found the depot. There were three bed frames available, but the problem was transport. A kind-hearted gentlemen who was in charge of the distribution of the furniture took pity on us. From somewhere he produced a wheelbarrow and helped us to load the bed frames onto it, but there was no room for the mattresses. Thus equipped, we set off and pushed the wheelbarrow across the streets of Prague, to our college. This took most of the day and when we unloaded the bed frames it was too late to go and fetch the mattresses. We assembled the beds, went out to find a shop where we could get some rolls and cheese which we ate on our return to our room. We went to the

Prague 1947. Eva on the left, me in the centre and Inge on my right.

kitchen, boiled some water and put a few leaves of tea we brought with us into the boiling water. We considered the drink to be tea, but it was so weak that it didn't taste of tea at all. We decided that this was a new drink, and invented a new name for it: 'kipiatok'.

After we had had a shower in the college's communal bathroom each of us wrapped herself in a blanket which we had brought with us, lay down on the bed frame, and fell asleep. Next morning we completed the furnishing of our room. We got the mattresses and two wardrobes which we transported to our college using the same means of transport we had used previously for the bed frames. Then we returned the wheelbarrow to the depot in Žižkov and exhausted, returned to our new home.

Just as we started to unpack our things a young attractive woman arrived with a man and a bed. 'I am Zdena,' she said, 'and I have been allotted space in this room which we will share. I hope you don't mind.' Inge, Eva and I introduced ourselves, and were quite pleased to have a 'native' for she was Czech and not Slovak, to share our room. It was obvious she was well organized, for her bed was brought in by a young man in a van together with all her possessions. Zdena shared the room with us for a whole year after which time she gave up her studies, left the college and we lost touch.

We were really pleased now, we had a home in Prague, and we were ready to start our studies. In the evening we met Rudi, who stayed in a room in college that he shared with another student.

Each morning we went to the University to enquire about our courses and what books we would need to obtain. We also applied and received a study grant, for none of us had any financial support. During these first few days we were so pre-occupied with sorting out the basic requirements for our new existence that we almost forgot to take in the beauty of the city we had decided to settle in.

Chapter 2

Our new home, Hradební Ulice, was in the old town and it was also close to the river, and nearby there were some boats for hire. Whenever we had time we rented a boat and rowed along the river Vltava. We could see the Castle and St. Vitus's Cathedral as we glided quietly under the bridges past the Národní Divadlo (National Theatre), the island opposite, and under the Charles Bridge that was built in the 15th century, and at that time was the only one to connect the two parts of the city that sprang up on the banks of the river Vltava. As we were becoming more familiar with Prague we were overjoyed and happy with our choice to settle here in Prague.

The Clock Tower in the centre of Prague.

Chapter 3

Glimpses Of Student Life

From left to right: Rudi, Eva, Anton and I in Prague 1948.

Student life.

There were at least 4,000 students, including us, enrolled to study medicine. Not only were Czech universities closed during the Nazi occupation of Bohemia and Moravia between 1939 and 1945, but in the effort to destroy the soul of the nation, many intellectuals, including university professors and lecturers were imprisoned, sent to concentration camps and killed. Now in 1945 the Universities had re-opened and students who had been unable to benefit from higher education for six years flooded towards the newly opened Charles University. But the Universities were understaffed and not equipped to cope with so many students. There was a shortage of books and teachers, and there were no lecture halls that could accommodate the large number of students. It was up to us students to cope with these shortcomings. The students' union building in Spálená Ulice, swarmed with enthusiastic young students who tried to deal with these problems. The atmosphere was exciting and as we were part of it we too tried to do our best.

I 'manned' an old discarded photocopying machine and spent hours photocopying old textbooks that either some people had donated to us or some students had found on the bookshelves in their parents' and relatives' homes. These copies were then distributed among the students. I particularly enjoyed looking at, and copying German anatomy atlases that depicted superb drawings of the human body prepared at the beginning of the 20th century by Johannes Sobotta. Some Czech teachers tried heroically to organize our efforts and to provide us with a proper medical course.

No lecture theatre at the University was big enough to accommodate 4,000 first year medical students. Therefore one of largest halls in Prague's cultural centre, Lucerna, had been 'requisitioned' by the new University authorities for teaching medical students. Although the lectures were helpful, a major problem, common to all medical and science students, was to acquire the necessary practical experience needed to properly understand the subject. Books and lectures were not sufficient and there were no facilities for laboratory practicals or for dissection of cadavers that would help us to acquire the necessary information we needed to become good doctors. I found it difficult to learn anatomy from books and pictures only and asked other students I met at lectures whether there was a place where we could find real human bones, or maybe even a skeleton to get a better three dimensional picture of the human body.

One student told me that the old curator at the medical school Mr. Purkrábek, had rescued some bones from the Germans when they ransacked the Czech medical school, and that he might be prepared to show us these bones. To impress Mr. Purkrábek I put on my best dress, a pale green silk one, and a matching cardigan and set out to visit the 'caretaker'. I went to the Anatomy Department, and was told that Mr. Purkrábek's office was in the basement. When I found him I was confronted by a short, grey haired man with a little moustache and a twinkle in his eye. He looked me up and down and I blushed under his gaze. Then he asked me why I had come to see him. I was somehow very shy, and explained that I was a medical student and would like to learn more anatomy, and that it would help me a lot if he could show me some human bones and skeletons. Mr. Purkrábek looked at me and growled: 'If I show you some bones you will not know what to do with them.' I had to agree that this was so, for I didn't even have a good text book with pictures of the bones. 'So what should I do to learn the anatomy of the body?' I asked. He took a look at me and after a few seconds said: 'I will teach you all there is to know about the human skeleton.

Come to this office every morning at seven o'clock and I will spend one hour with you demonstrating the different bones, and showing you how they are joined together at joints. Also I will show you where the muscles are attached to the bones to move them.' Mr. Purkrábek never told me or other students much about himself, but there were rumours that when the Germans came to confiscate all the teaching materials of the University, Mr. Purkrábek removed all the specimens and bones to a secret hiding place where they were not found. He never handed anything over to the Germans, and apparently pretended not to know where all the material had disappeared to. In this way he rescued valuable material, which he now used to teach us, the new generation of Czech doctors.

The next morning at seven o'clock sharp I turned up at Mr. Purkrábek's office and found that about six other students were also waiting for him to attend his demonstration. When he arrived we went to his little room and listened attentively to his introductory talk. After this first lesson, we assembled every morning in his dingy office in the basement where he had carefully prepared a selection of bones for us to study. His lectures were clear and lucid and he was able to convey a fantastic amount of information in the short time he spent with us. True to his promise he taught us how to recognize the features of particular bones, how they were connected to each other and where the tendons of muscles that moved the joints were attached to the bones. His teaching sessions were remarkable also by the fact that he could make a rather boring subject exciting, and inspired us to see the beauty as well as the efficiency of the way the human body is constructed and designed to perform all the necessary functions.

Gradually Eva, Inge and I settled into a routine. During the day we attended classes, and in the evenings we got together with Rudi and other friends. We had great hopes that we now would have a chance to build a new world, which would be free and just. The only problem we had was to decide how to go about this task and for a while we believed that the Communist Party would show us the way.

Rudi was the first in our group of four to join the Communist Party. The evening after he joined the party we met in a small restaurant where we ordered some meat in a dill sauce and dumplings (koprová omáčka s knedlíkem) and while eating this typical Czech meal, we discussed his decision. Eva was the most skeptical. 'Why did you join?' she challenged Rudi, and continued: 'I have heard so many terrible things from my parents about what happened in Hungary when the communists came to power for a brief period after the First World War. There were lootings, killings, pogroms and unspeakable violence. A communist system does not seem to promise a better future.' Rudi did think about it and replied: 'All these bad things happened after the end of a terrible war, when people took advantage of the political upheaval and acted badly. But it was not the fault of the communists. Now here in Czechoslovakia we have a democracy, and the Communist Party is one of many. The program of the party is most appealing and the scientific analysis of social problems of capitalist societies by Marx and Engels seem to highlight the reality and injustices of the capitalist society. Can you remember the Munich Agreement, how our capitalist allies betrayed us and sold our small country to the Germans? So what is the choice?' Rudi was most convincing and although I tended to agree with him, our discussions went on for weeks, until finally by the end of 1946, Inge and I too, decided to join the Party. To be accepted for party membership we had to apply and be interviewed. In my case the interview panel consisted of four students my own age, or maybe a bit older. It was held in one of the rooms of the Student Union in Spálená. The room was very barren and ugly. The panel sat behind a wooden table and I sat on a chair facing them. 'Why do you want to join the Communist Party?' was the first question. My answer was, 'It promises a more just and fair society, where everyone can share in the wealth of the country. Everyone will have the same chance, no matter what his or her race or class origin is, or how much money the family had.' 'Have you read any communist literature?' came the next question. 'Yes, *Marx, Das Kapital.*' My answer seemed to impress the committee and I was offered party membership then and there. I was told that I will be sent the address and time of the next meeting which I will then be able to attend.

I left and went home pleased with myself and certain that I had made the right decision. Back in our room at college I told Inge and Eva: 'I have joined the Communist Party. Everyone I met was very nice, and I think I did the right thing.' Inge joined the party shortly after me. For a while life continued uneventfuly. We studied, went to lectures and met many other students and our social life started to be more active. There were several parties organized by young men from other colleges and just before Chrismas 1946 we girls from the college in Hradební Ulice were invited to one of these. The party was in a college in Dejvice, and almost all the girls from our college decided to go. We didn't have smart party clothes, but a dark skirt and white blouse seemed to have been quite satisfactory. Inge, Eva and I all put on this attire, which looked a bit like a uniform. With the rest of the college girls we took the tram to Dejvice and followed all the crowds to the room where loud music was playing and people were already dancing.

It was a really lovely room, spacious and bright. There was a small orchestra of amateur musicians who played jazz. We sat around on chairs, with a glass of wine each and watched the dancing couples. A shy boy came and asked me to dance with him. 'I can't really dance' I explained, 'I never had a chance to learn to dance.' But I joined the boy, he introduced himself and said that his name was Ota Šik. He too was a medical student. We went to the dance floor and moved about following the rhythm of the music. It was a pleasant feeling to have physical contact with a boy and feel our bodies moving together. Inge and Eva also danced with boys, and we all enjoyed ourselves. As the evening went on, people were gradually leaving the hall, until there was only Eva, Inge and I with our dancing partners left in the hall. I was surprised, because I didn't see anyone leave the building. I asked Ota where everyone was. He gave me an amused look: 'I will show you,' he said, took me by the hand and walked up the corridor where the bedrooms were. He opened one door, and I just caught a glimpse of a boy and girl undressed in bed. Then in the corridor, Ota tried to kiss me on the mouth, and invited me to his room. I was shocked: 'But I don't know you,' I said. 'Well you know me now,' Ota said. I pulled away from him and ran downstairs to the big hall, where by now the music had stopped our dancing partners had disappeared and only Inge, Eva and I remained sitting on hard wooden chairs in the empty room. It was late, the heating had gone off, and there were no trams or buses running any more, so we sat shivering till next morning. At dawn, as soon as the trams started to run we returned to our college, dead tired and disappointed. We went to bed, and slept. When we woke up and went out of our room to take a shower, we found a big notice nailed on our door which said: NURSERY. So this was how our colleagues thought of us and there was some truth in it. The three of us were immature and had not acquired the social skills of a twenty year old person. This was not surprising, for, during the war, we had missed several years of social contact with people of our age.

Time passed, we studied, and tried to develop our personal lives. In my case it was mainly working out my relationship with Rudi. I felt uncertain about him and was not sure how well I knew him. Meanwhile Rudi managed to acquire a small flat in the centre of Prague, and I often visited him there. It was rather a luxury to have a room just to himself, and we were lucky that it gave us an opportunity to get to know each other more intimately. I was disappointed for somehow our sexual experiences were not very enjoyable, probably for either of us. I was convinced that this was all my fault, my lack of experience and possibly insufficient love for Rudi. I think we both believed that our understanding of each other and affection we felt for each other would improve things. We carried on in this way for quite a while without any noticeable changes in our relationship.

Meanwhile, Inge and Eva also found boy friends; Eva fell in love with Rudi's best friend Anton (Tono) and Inge became involved with Bubo, a boy from Slovakia, who, like Inge, was studying chemical engineering. Unfortunaley he seemed to be always sick and needed much attention, which Inge wholeheartedly gave him.

Visit to Hungary.

During our first student summer holiday, at the beginning of August 1946, I travelled to Budapest to visit some of my aunts and uncles who had survived the war. I was curious to see Budapest again, the city that I had left just over a year ago and I wanted to know how my family had settled into the new post war life. My train from Prague arrived at the Nyugati Station where trains coming from the West usually arrived. Although the station hadn't changed since I had last seen it over a year previously, when I was leaving by train to Bratislava to return to Trnava, it was only now that I was amazed by its grandeur. My Aunt Manci was waiting for me on the platform. Manci was a very important person for me. When I was a child she was my favourite Aunt. She was always interested in me, taught me swimming and encouraged my interests in reading and poetry. During the war, when my parents and I had to flee Slovakia to avoid being deported to the concentration camps and lived as refugees in Budapest, she tried to make my stay there less lonely and enjoyable by taking me to exhibitions, swimming pools and arranging other activities for me. I had not seen her since I left Budapest in May 1945. Now when I saw her again, she looked smart as usual, but more content. I fell into her arms, she held me close to her and I felt a tiny bit like coming home. Then she held me at arms length and surveyed my appearance. 'Gerti, you look well,' she said to me, 'but we have to get you some smarter clothes'. This was the problem with my family, they always wanted me to be well dressed, and I didn't care at all and thought it was a waste of time.

Manci's flat was only a few minutes walk from the station in a small street called appropriately Alig Utza (which translated, means: *hardly a street*). It branched off a large road called Váci Ut. As we walked along Váci Ut, I couldn't help but compare beautiful Prague, unblemished by the war, to Budapest, so badly scarred by the fighting. This was depressing and brought back so many horrifying memories of my war-time experiences, so that I almost wished I hadn't come. Yet when I held onto Manci's arm and she pressed her hand against my elbow I knew I needed this family contact very badly. We arrived at her home which was in an apartment block, where my Uncle Arthur and Aunt Ada lived in a flat on the first floor and Manci with her husband Andor in a flat on the second floor.

The house had been built just before the war and it belonged to my uncle Arthur. Arthur was my mother's oldest brother. My mother and her family had lived in a small village in Slovakia (Slovenský Meder), which was then part of the Austro-Hungarian Hapsburg Empire. My mother's parents owned a grocery shop, but the proceeds of the shop could not cover adaequately the expenses involved in having to care for 13 children and the family was rather poor. Arthur, the oldest of the children, left his native small village at the age of 17 to try his luck in the big city: Budapest. He was a very astute business man, opened a textile factory and became rich. My mother, his youngest sister was a great favourite of his and this affection for her, was transferred to me. He married my father's sister Ada so I was a blood relative to both of them. The house Arthur had built, and where he and Manci now lived with their families, contained about 20 apartments. The outside hadn't been damaged during the war, since it was in a tiny little street off the main road, and it looked quite grandiose with two sculptures of lions that flanked the stairs that led to a rather ornate metal gate. The entrance hall was bright and spacious and the lift very modern. We took the lift to the second floor and Manci led the way to her flat. Manci's husband Andor was waiting for us and so was her maid, Maria who lived in Manci's flat and helped with the housework, because Manci now had a full time job as a translator from Hungarian to Russian and vice-versa.

As soon as we arrived Manci telephoned my Aunt Ada and Uncle Arthur who lived on the first floor, to tell them that I had arrived, and both of them came up to Manci's flat. They looked well and it was wonderful to be surrounded by family. We were eager to hear news about each other. I gave an account of my experiences in Prague and told of my new life there and how much I enjoyed my studies.

Of course the main topic of our conversation was remembering those members of the family who were missing and had not survived the Holocaust, among them my parents and both my grandmothers. For me these recollections were very painful, for I still couldn't quite get used to the idea that I would never see my parents and grandmothers again. Yet, here I was with members of my family who had survived, and there was comfort in the fact that they had. We had a modest meal together, for there were food shortages and rationing in Budapest, and then Aunt Ada and Uncle Arthur returned to their flat on the first floor, Andor went to bed. Manci and I stayed up and talked.

Manci filled me in with details about their lives in Budapest: 'Gerti, for the first time in my life I have a job. I can't tell you how happy that makes me.' I could see from her expression that she really enjoyed her work. She continued: 'Andor, cannot work, his eyesight has deteriorated so much that he can barely see.' So Manci was the breadwinner. Ada and Arthur didn't work. Arthur's textile factory which had been a very lucrative enterprise before the war, was taken over during the German occupation by the fascists and had been nationalized when the communists came to power after the war. Arthur felt too old to start something new. Ada resumed her previous life of leisure and Arthur joined her. They played bridge, met friends and wasted time.

It was a lovely mild, warm evening and Manci and I went for a walk. I wanted to see Budapest again. We walked to the main street St. István Körút, and then towards the Danube where the Margaret Bridge (Margit Híd) used to be. Only the remains of the bridge that had been destroyed before the Germans left Budapest were visible. It was still impossible to cross the Danube here and get to the Margaret Island (Margit Sziget) or to Buda. Everything was shabby and tawdry and yet there were many people on the streets and some were sitting at tables outside coffee bars drinking something that smelled of coffee. Were these some signs of recovery? We too sat down and had 'espresso coffee' which to me tasted really good.

Next day, I was taken to a dressmaker, for both my aunts decided that I looked very shabby and even in my modest luggage that consisted of a small suitcase there wasn't a decent dress or coat. My aunts somehow found a place where they could buy lovely silk material and some cotton print. We took the purchase to the dressmaker and two new dresses were to be made for me. One smart silk dress, and one cotton dress. The dressmaker was a middle aged lady, and was very impressed by my proportions. She took the measurements and with great enthusiasm took on the task of making me look respectable.

I spent most of the time in Budapest with my family, but I did make time to take advantage of the many swimming pools and spas that were functioning. I also walked a lot and visited places where I had lived during the war with my parents. To get a better idea how people lived in post war Budapest I visited other friends I knew from before the war. I found my French teacher who had saved my life in 1944 and still lived in the same place. She was very poor, for no one was taking French lessons any more and she had lost her meagre savings during the war and post war currency changes. It was sad to see her in such dire circumstances.

Then I visited my cousin Baby with whom I had stayed during the last few months my parents and I were in Hungary and where I had worked as a nanny, helping to look after her three children. Baby, her husband and children had survived the war and lived in their old luxurious villa, which was not luxurious any more. During the war when the Germans occupied Hungary their beautiful villa was used to house some German officers, who did all they could to ruin the place. Nevertheless, this was insignifcant compared to the loss of Baby's mother and grandmother, my aunt Kate, both of whom died in the gas chambers of Auschwitz. When I arrived at Baby's house, she welcomed me with a warm hug, and took me to the kitchen, where we brewed some drink that was supposed to be tea. Then we sat down at the kitchen table. We were alone in the house, the children had gone to a swimming pool and Baby's husband, Imre, was trying to restore his factory, which had been nationalized but the government needed his help to run it. I couldn't wait to tell Baby about my life in Prague, and I also couldn't conceal my enthusiasm about the great efforts we in Czechoslovakia, were making to build a just communist society. 'I have joined the Communist Party and we are going to change the world,' I blurted out. Baby looked at me with her huge blue eyes and after a few seconds of silence said: 'Gerti, I know you are young and you need to believe that it is possible to build a just and decent society, but I am sure that communism is not the road to it. Look at the Soviet Union, look at the soldiers who fought for our liberation and died in their thousands. When they came here victorious we realized that they had never had a wrist watch, for they stole as many wrist watches as they could from us, and decorated both their arms from the wrists to the arm pits with them. They had never seen indoor bathrooms and toilets, and didn't know what a toothbrush or toothpaste was and above all they had no respect for human life not even their own. What kind of society is it that after 30 years still has millions of citizens like this? It must be an evil regime that does not seem to be able to look after the most basic needs of its citizens, and I for one cannot imagine that a communist system will work here or anywhere else.' I tried to argue: 'In the Soviet Union there was such poverty and lack of education, when people started on their road to Socialism, so maybe that there just wasn't enough time to achieve their goals. Here and particularly in Czechoslovakia it is different. We have a tradition of democracy, a good industrial economic basis, and a very well educated population. Don't you think we have the possibility of building a socialist country where all the people can share the wealth of the country and have an equal chance to prosper? Also, in the recent democratic elections in

Czechoslovakia the Socialist parties had a majority, so it is the wish of the majority of the people in Czechoslovakia to have a socialist society.' So I regurgitated all the propaganda they fed us at party meetings. Baby held my hand, and became quite sad: 'I really do not want to shatter your illusions, but I do not believe it is possible even in your country to have a successful communist regime. First, it means that there will be a dictatorship, struggle for power, which brings out the worst in people. And then I do not believe that it is natural for people to share resources. Also people really are not equal, and you have to accept that everyone has different abilities and talents. You cannot deny that. You, for example, survived the war because of your vitality, desire to live and the special skills you employed to achieve that. But most of your Jewish friends and family members did not survive. So each individual is different and one cannot make them equal by declaring them to be equal. It is quite unnatural, and it cannot work and make people happy.'

Baby's children came home, and I was delighted to see them again. Mayo, the oldest was very beautiful, and Daisy mischievous, as I remembered her. Bencze, the youngest was a toddler and very charming. They were a happy family, and did not deserve the hardships they were to encounter in the next few years when Hungary became a communist dictatorship. Baby's weariness of the nature of communism proved very much justified.

I left the villa and walked back to my Aunt's house in Pest. It was a long walk, for the only bridge that connected Buda to Pest was far from my Aunt's house. As I was walking I thought about the different attitude of Baby to that of Manci, who was full of enthusiasm for the new socialist order. Nevertheless, Baby's arguments left a deep impression on me and I was confused; for the first time since I joined the Communist Party I had real doubts whether this was the right way to go about building a new society.

On my return I told Manci about my discussion with Baby, and that I felt uncertain about my membership of the Communist Party. 'Gerti,' Manci said, 'you have to follow your convictions, you may be wrong, but just wait and see. We are all biased after our experiences with the fascists, we wish to create something completely different. Whether communism will be the answer, I really do not know. Just keep an open mind.' I stopped worrying about it, and enjoyed the simple warmth of being with my family.

Shortly before my departure we went to the dressmaker to pick up my new dresses. They turned out really well and I couldn't wait to flaunt them in front of my friends in Prague. Rudi particularly liked me to be well dressed, but unfortunately this did not happen very often. My holiday in Hungary was drawing to an end. At the end of August I packed my suitcase, which was now really full. Manci came with me to the train station and I took the train first to Bratislava where I was to meet Rudi and his mother.

The journey to Bratislava was relatively short, only four hours. I found a window seat in a compartment which was quite empty. My memories surfaced as the train travelled through the familiar landscape and the places where, not so long ago, I had crossed the border between Slovakia and Hungary illegally with my mother. Just over a year ago I made the same journey to Bratislava and then on to my home town, Trnava. The war was over and I was hoping then that my parents had survived the war and would return home. But after weeks and months of waiting, they did not return from the concentration camps they had been taken to, and I was alone.

Now here I was, more than a year later making the same journey, realizing that in spite of the fact that I had made a new start and had some purpose in my life, the wounds caused by the loss of my parents had not healed. Would my parents have approved of my choices and my new life?

Back in Prague.

In September I was happy to be back in Prague, in our college in Hradební Ulice. The term started and my friends and I were together again. It gave me great comfort to celebrate our reunion and we went out for dinner, to a rather reasonably priced restaurant in the Old Town. The food was not very good, but because of the rationing and food shortages it was a special treat to have a meal prepared for us. I arrived in my new silk dress from Budapest. Everyone admired me and Rudi gave me a big hug and kissed me on the mouth: 'Gerti, you should always dress like this. You have a lovely body, and this dress really shows it.' I was in fact quite upset about the comment, for I felt that it shouldn't really matter what I looked like. If Rudi loved me as a person, he should love me whatever my appearance. But he wanted to show me off. The others also joined in and praised my appearance. Inge and Eva also had new dresses, that they had acquired during the summer holiday but even I had to admit that mine was the smartest. My aunts and the dressmaker in Budapest really had done a good job. We exchanged experiences of our respective summer holidays. Inge had spent her time in Trnava, helping her mother to settle in their old flat, where she now lived alone and which I remembered so well. She admitted: 'It is really difficult for my mother to live among all those people who would gladly have handed her over to be taken to Auschwitz. I felt really uncomfortable in Trnava, and couldn't wait to come back to Prague.' Eva spent the summer in her home town Nitra and her reaction to being at 'home' was similar to that of Inge. 'I cannot believe that Nitra is my home.' Eva said. Rudi spent the summer in Bratislava with his friends from Auschwitz, Freddie Wetzler, Anton Rosen and Czeszlaw Mordowicz, all of whom escaped from Auschwitz in a similar way to Rudi. These experiences formed a very strong bond between the four of them. Eva's and Inge's recent boyfriends, Anton and Bubo, spent the summer in their respective homes with the surviving members of their family. All of us were happy that we had chosen to live in Prague and not Slovakia.

How did we spend our time in the second year of our studies? We worked hard, and it was not easy to study with so little help from our teachers and so few resources. The lectures were given in a large lecture hall and that made them very impersonal, and we had access to only a few books. Altogether, my studies were not very exciting, and I was getting bored.

One afternoon, while I was trying to find a book on biology in a second-hand bookshop I came across a book that was to influence my entire future. It was in German written by a Swiss physiologist called von Muralt and was called, *The Transmission of Signals in Nerves (Die Signalübermittlung im Nerven)*. I bought the book, which had a lovely blue cover, and returned home to show it to Inge and Eva. When I tried to read it I realized that I didn't understand any of it, and yet I was determined that one day I would understand how the nervous system analyses the signals that it receives from the outside world.

The second year of our studies ended and our summer vacation started. This holiday was rather special, for Czechoslovakia hosted the first World Festival of Democratic Youth and Students (WFDYS). The World Federation of Democratic Youth had decided to celebrate its first Festival in our country in remembrance of the events of October and November 1939, when thousands of young Czechs rose to demontrate against the occupation of their country by Nazi Germany. This caused a wave of repression that included the closing of Universities and the arrest of 1,850 students as well as the internment of 1,200 in Nazi concentration camps. The Festival was also meant to pay tribute to the Czech cities of Lidice and Lezáky which were eradicated by the Nazis as a retribution for the assassination of Reinhard Heydrich, the brutal governor of Bohemia and Moravia, also nicknamed 'The Butcher of Prague', by the Czech people.

For us students, the staging of the Festival in Prague was a momentous event and we threw ourselves into helping to organise it with much enthusiasm. Almost 20,000 foreign young people from 71 different countries were expected to participate. To provide accommodation, food and facilities for different performances, and interpreters for the leading members of the various delegations was a mammoth task, and its success was partly due to government support but also to the hard work of young people. Finally on the

25th July 1947 the Festival opened at Strahov Stadium (Velký Strahovský Stadion), which at the time was one of the biggest stadiums in the world. The stadium is situated on top of a hill called Petřín and boasts magnificent views of the old city of Prague as well as the Castle. In this beautiful setting, in the presence of 17,000 young people, the blue flag with the emblem of the WFDY was raised and for the first time the song of Democratic Youth composed by the Russian composer Novikov, which was to be the anthem of the WFDY, was heard. The slogan of the Festival was: 'Youth unite, forward for lasting peace.' Standing there at the opening ceremony at the Strahov Stadium I completely succumbed to the mood and enthusiasm of the participants. Here we were, the new generation changing the world and creating a new future and lasting peace together with all the young people on earth. It was a wonderful feeling, and we were doubly proud that it was happening in our country.

Apart from watching some magnificent performances brought to us by young artists from around the world, I was given the job of interpreter to some delegates to help them to get around Prague and meet up with other young people. I had a reasonably good knowledge of French, so I was initially assigned to some young people from some Arab-speaking countries who were more fluent in French than Russian or English. This included members of the Egyptian, Palestinian, Morrocan and Algerian delegation.

One afternoon shortly after the beginning of the Festival, I was given the task of picking up a group of young delegates from Arab countries, and showing them our city. They were staying in a student hostel in Dejvice, and I went to meet them. Six unusually smartly dressed men waited for me outside the hostel. I introduced myself, told them that I was to help them to get to know Prague. I planned to show them the beauty of our city. I explained my plan to them and we started off on our walk towards the Castle and St. Vitus's Cathedral, a short pleasant walk from Dejvice.

I had done my homework and tried to act as a proper guide, explaining the style and architecture of the buildings and their special significance for our Czech history. Not only did none of the delegates show any interest, but they kept interrupting me and making it clear that they did not want to see Prague, or talk to me. One of them asked: 'Where could we get some vodka?' and when I said that I thought Muslims were not allowed to drink alcohol, they replied that they are atheists. One of them had an even more peculiar request: 'Instead of all this sightseeing, could you introduce us to some pretty blonde girls that would be prepared to go to bed with us. Perhaps you could take us to a place where we could meet some girls.' I looked at them in amazement, this surely was not in the spirit of the Festival. I told them that such a task is far beyond my duties as an interpreter, and in any case I don't know of any such place. They laughed at me and told me to go away since I was quite useless to them. I tried to argue with them, and explain that the true purpose of the Festival was to discuss common problems of young people throughout the world and to understand each others' cultures, but they found this very amusing, and laughed. Eventually, disappointed, I left them on top of the Castle Hill. I was so full of ideas that the Festival had been arranged to bring people who think alike together, and to help to understand their different cultures that this lewd request to find some girls to sleep with, really shook me. I couldn't even see the funny side of this and all I wanted to do was distance myself from these people.

At the time I didn't consider it as a warning that our ideals of peace and friendship may not persist in the real world, where the values of some of delegates were so different from mine and from what I expected from peace loving young people. I was too idealistic to admit to myself that some of the cultural differences may be unsurmountable. I avoided the Arab delegates for the rest of the Festival, and never found out whether they bedded some pretty blonde girls during their stay in Prague.

Although this experience dampened my enthusiasm, it did not prevent me from enjoying the rest of the Festival. We met and talked to young people from South America and listened to their accounts of their struggle for freedom and democracy. Delegates from Black Africa talked about their problems of obtaining independence from foreign rule and our European friends discussed how best to build a new and fair society from the ruins of the Second World War. Many countries sent dance groups and the vivid music and dance of some of the African groups made a deep impression on me. There were several outstanding performances from young Russian musicians and these increased our sympathies for a country that we believed freed us from fascism and we thought how wonderful it must be to have such talented young artists.

The Festival lasted for almost four weeks and when it ended we were exhausted and ready just to rest before our new term started in September. The third year of my medical studies was more interesting. We started to learn more about pathology and malfunction of the body. I was lucky to get a place in the pathology department of one of Prague's large district hospitals (Bulovka) which had a wonderful chief, Dr. Gross. He liked teaching and showed us not only how to recognise various alterations in the tissues caused by disease in the bodies we dissected, but organised sessions with clinicians who treated the patients before they died and discussed with us the symptoms they had and the treatment they received while they were under their care. This helped us to understand many conditions which later on we saw in the wards. I enjoyed my studies during this year, and was determined to become a good doctor. We were now seasoned students, and the year passed very quickly.

Trip to Poland.

In the summer of 1948 a group of Czechoslovak students went to Poland for a trip. Rudi and I joined the group, but Inge and Eva didn't come. We were excited about the trip, for we hoped to spend some time at the Baltic Sea. Czechoslovakia is a landlocked country and neither Rudi nor I had ever seen the sea.

There were about twelve of us travelling. We took the train from Prague's central station, sat on hard wooden benches, and watched the landscape as the train took us across Moravia, Slovakia and into Poland. The journey took over fourteen hours and part of it was overnight. We slept in our seats, and didn't mind the discomfort. Early in the morning we arrived at our first stop, Krakow, where two Polish students were waiting to show us around the city.

Chapter 3

Krakow, like Prague, was not damaged during the war and is a lovely city. After our sightseeing, when we were quite exhausted other Polish students joined us and we sat in the magnificent Town Square outside the cathedral and sang folksongs. One of the girls in our group, a medical student called Eliana had a beautiful voice and enchanted us all with her singing. We were then taken to a student hostel, and shared a very drab dormitory for about 20 people. We were all in the same room, boys and girls together.

Rudi and I had our beds next to each other, we pushed them together, huddled up together, and enjoyed feeling each other's warmth, but the dormitory was too crowded for more intimate contact, and we lay still, exhausted and soon fell asleep.

The following morning we boarded a train in Krakow that took us to Warsaw. We arrived in Warsaw in the afternoon. I don't think any of us were prepared to see the devastation and ruins that was Warsaw. There were no buildings where we could be accommodated for the night, so our Polish fellow students put up some tents for us on what we thought were the outskirts of Warsaw. They provided us with sleeping bags and we went to sleep. We had no idea which part of Warsaw we were staying in for everything looked the same, just remnants of houses and rubble.

A good looking Polish medical student called Zigmond picked us up in the morning and took us on a guided tour through the ruins of Warsaw, which he did not treat with equal reverence. He pointed out the place where the Old City used to be on the banks of the Vistula river. There were remnants of old buildings among the rubble and he proudly announced that the Old City would be completely rebuilt and restored to look the same as before the war. Then in a different part of the city, he pointed out some rubble which to us, didn't look different from the rest of the rubble, and commented: 'This was the Ghetto, where the Warsaw Jews were killed by the Germans during their uprising. The only good thing Hitler did.' In present-day Warsaw this site is remembered by a special memorial that honours the heroes of the Jewish uprising, where a handful of starved Jews managed to fight the Germans and hold out for a whole month before they were defeated and killed. After Zigmond's comment I stood there with my mouth open, worried that Rudi would attack Zigmond. But we were too well behaved as visitors, and just turned back to find our tent. Our whole group of Czechoslovak students was so stunned by this remark that our elated mood vanished, and we just wanted to get away from Warsaw, away from Poland. How was it possible that barely three years after the war, with the memories of what the Germans did to Jews and Poles so recent, a young Polish student could make a comment like that? Is the anti-Semitism and inhumanity so deeply ingrained that an 'educated' person cannot understand what happened here?

Fortunately, the next day we left Warsaw and continued our journey to Gdańsk (Danzig) where Rudi and three other Czech students were to work at the Engineering Department of the University and we, medical students, were assigned for work in the ruins of a hospital.

The very first thing we did on our arrival to Gdańsk was to go to the sea. It was an incredible experience to see the harbour and the sea, the great ships that could travel anywhere in the world. A sea port is like a door to the world, through which one can step out and reach the most exotic and exciting places. I felt then that there is a special magic about the sea and a great port, and succumbed to it completely. Even today, after I have travelled to so many different places, I love being in a port and by the sea.

Finally we were accompanied by our hosts to a ruin of a hostel where we were to stay for three weeks. Next morning we medical students reported to the hospital. The hospital lacked almost everything, including qualified doctors, but was nevertheless overcrowded with patients. The senior doctor, trying to do his best to cope with a desperate situation, asked each of us how much we knew and what we were doing at our medical school in Prague. I said that I was interested in neurology, but soon regretted having said this. I was sent to a neurology ward and just one week after having arrived I was asked to carry out a lumbar puncture on an elderly male patient. This is a procedure where one inserts a large needle into the cavity of the vertebral column and withdraw some fluid from this cavity. There is an element of risk, for an inexperienced person, and I certainly was that, could put the needle in the wrong place, damage the spinal cord and cause paralysis. I didn't dare to refuse this request from a senior member of the staff, went to the library where I found a few books, read everything I could find about how to perform a lumbar puncture, and next day with jittery knees I successfully performed one.

During our student years in Prague, none of us medical students had had any hands-on experience with patients, but this changed in Gdańsk where we were given far too much access and responsibility for caring for patients, and often had to cope with situations we could not handle very well.

We were compensated for all this hard work by the excitement of being close to the Baltic Sea. Almost every day we found time to go to the beach, in the nearby resort of Sopot that had a magnificent sandy beach and was just a short bus ride from Gdańsk. We hurled ourselves into the sea and savoured a completely new sensation, so unique for us coming from a landlocked country, to swim in salt water for the first time in our lives. We also strolled along the soft sand on the beach looking for ambers that were quite abundant in the sand. I collected enough of them to bring home and make a necklace. On the whole we had a wonderful time. Rudi and I enjoyed each others' company more then ever before, and it was during this holiday that we decided to get married.

Rudi and I in 1947.

Chapter 4
Getting Married

'Our' place called *Kampa* in Prague.

Rudi and I often walked along the banks of the river Vltava near the Charles Bridge. Our favourite stop was a bench on the little island under the Charles Bridge, called *Kampa*. We considered the bench to be ours. On hot summer days the horse chestnut trees provided us with shade, and on other occasions they just looked pretty. In the spring their flowers were white and purple and we could not imagine a more beautiful place anywhere. Here I was happy to be with Rudi, my very handsome and clever friend. Sitting on our bench by the river Vltava with Rudi reminded me of the difficult times during the war when the two of us were watching a different river flow by. In the summer of 1944 in Bratislava when Rudi returned to Slovakia after having escaped from Auschwitz we often met at the banks of the Danube. It was here that he told me about the death camps and his fantastic escape. He talked with great passion during these meetings about the German plans, to kill half a million Hungarian Jews, that he had discovered while he was in Auschwitz. He was obsessed by his duty to warn the Hungarian Jews about this and tell them the truth about Auschwitz which was certain death. It was this knowledge about the plans of the Germans to exterminate the Hungarian Jews which prompted him and his friend Freddie Wetzler to attempt their dangerous and heroic escape. Rudi was, rightly, hoping that if the Hungarian Jews would know what to expect, their massacre would be prevented.

I now recall the intensity of my love for Rudi then. I admired his courage and resourcefulness that enabled him to escape the hell on earth that was Auschwitz, and I had a great desire to make him happy to compensate for all his suffering. I shared his passion to let the world know of the mass murder so as to save as many lives as possible from being slaughtered by the Germans. Then in Bratislava, I yearned to be touched by him and wanted him to make love to me. Now, here in Prague it was different. Sitting next to Rudi and watching another river, the Vltava, flow by, I didn't feel the same desire for physical contact and intimacy which we so easily could have shared.

Unlike most students who lived in shared accommodation, Rudi was privileged for he had a room all to himself. Nevertheless, we rarely went to Rudi's room, where we had all the privacy we could wish for. His room was part of a large flat in the centre of Prague, and we could have spent many nights together. Yet, we rarely did so, for when we were alone together in Rudi's room and made love, there was something strangely missing. There was a trace of violence in the way Rudi made love to me that scared and inhibited me. Rather than longing for physical contact I was afraid of it, and avoided it. One night I tried to discuss our problem with him: 'Rudi, could you be more tender and gentle when we are together?' I asked. But Rudi found it difficult to accept any suggestions that our lovemaking was unsatisfactory and persuaded me that it was all my fault, not being passionate enough and very inexperienced. That certainly was true, and I convinced myself that if we married and lived together, this small flaw in our relationship would correct itself. After all, everything else in our relationship was perfect. All our friends considered us a perfect couple. Rudi's mother Ilonka too believed that we were happy, and was enthusiastically championing our future marriage.

One Sunday afternoon during the autumn of 1948 when both Rudi and I were well seasoned students and ready for a change in our lives, we were walking on Petřín, a hill just to the left of the Castle. The leaves on the trees were changing colour, and the golden glow of the tree tops made the hill look like a cathedral with a gilded roof. There was a very nice restaurant (Nebozízek) on top of the hill with spectacular views over the city. It was late afternoon and Rudi and I went to have tea there, though it was beyond our means, for it was very expensive, but we felt like doing something extravagant. We sat down outside on a verandah and ordered tea and cakes. And then suddenly Rudi said: 'Gerti, I would like us to get married soon and live together properly.' I was delighted that Rudi said this, for I too wanted to be married to Rudi and share my life with him completely. So I replied: 'I think this is a great idea; I too would like us to get married. 'Shall I tell my mother about our decision?' asked Rudi, 'she will be delighted and will want to help to organize our wedding.' I thought about this, and then said: 'Perhaps we should tell her in person when we visit her at Christmas. I think it will be nicer to tell her rather then just write to her, or telephone her.'

Ilonka really tried to make me feel welcome in her home, and treated me as part of the family. During the Christmas break in 1948 when Rudi and I visited her in Bratislava she welcomed me in her flat and all the arrangements for my stay there were ready. A pleasant small room was set up for me and she prepared delicious meals for Rudi and myself. She understood how lonely I must have felt and tried to lessen the hurt I felt that both my parents perished in the Holocaust and that I was the only surviving member of our immediate family. Most other students went home to spend Christmas with their closest family members, but I had no parents, and spent Christmas with Rudi and his mother. Rudi's mother's understanding and love for me, helped to assuage the loneliness. Rudi was part of my life already, and an important link to my childhood and Trnava, where we grew up together.

Shortly after we arrived in Bratislava and settled in Ilonka Néni's flat Rudi said to her: 'Gerti and I have decided to get married, and I hope you will be pleased with this decision.' Ilonka's face lit up, and her blue eyes sparkled: 'It is about time,' she said, 'I have been waiting for this to happen for ages. Will you let me organize your wedding?' I gave her a hug, and felt comforted and reassured being held in her strong arms. 'Ilonka, the arrangements for our wedding could not be in better hands then yours. Many thanks.' Our wedding was planned to take place during the Easter break in April 1949. Ilonka, undertook all the preparations for the occasion with great enthusiasm, and insisted that we should get married in Bratislava. We were pleased that the preparations were to be taken care of by her, for we knew that in view of her efficiency all the arrangements would work perfectly. Shortly after Christmas we sent out invitations for our wedding to our close friends. They included Inge and Eva, and Anthony, and Laco who were Rudi's comrades while he fought as a Partisan, and with whom he shared the tent they slept in. Also Freddie Wetzler, with whom Rudi escaped from Auschwitz, and the other two Auschwitz escapees, Czeszlaw Mordowicz and Anton Rosen were invited to our wedding. Rudi's step-sister Fanči her husband and two sons Stefan and Jan were also invited. I had no one from my family who could attend the wedding; my Hungarian relatives were unable to come, and my cousins in Slovakia did not show much interest in my life. I missed my parents and wondered whether I had rushed into marriage because of the loneliness I felt all the time.

After New Years' Eve, in January 1949 we went back to Prague to continue our life there. I tried not to think about what life would be like after we got married, but some preparations had to be made for our future as a married couple. Above all, we needed to find a place where Rudi and I could live together, and in view of the extreme shortage of flats this was no easy task. However, because Rudi had been a Partisan, he enjoyed some privileges and managed to get a small one-bedroom flat for us in Dejvice, a pleasant suburb of Prague, close to the Castle and with easy access to the centre of Prague. Furnishing the flat was a problem, but we were able to buy a bed and some simple furniture. We were now prepared for our life together. At Easter 1949 we travelled to Bratislava, ready to get married. For the wedding ceremony I had planned to wear a navy suit with a white blouse. Ilonka Néni bought Rudi a very smart outfit and he looked dashing. To complete our preparations a few days before the wedding, Rudi and I went to a jeweller and bought two gold wedding rings.

The night before the wedding I was deeply disturbed, and cried most of the night. Although I was inexperienced and young, I knew that there was something missing in our relationship, and that neither Rudi nor I were ready to commit ourselves to living together. I shared a room with Eva and she heard me crying. I confided in her and told her of my fears. She tried to calm me and argued that probably most people were worried before taking on such a serious commitment as marriage. But her arguments did not help to soothe my anxiety and worries about our future.

On the 16th of April 1949 we had a civic wedding ceremony in the office of Bratislava's Town Hall, where Rudi and I took the usual marriage vows and made promises I hoped we would keep. I was told by my friends that at the wedding I looked smart in my simple but rather well cut dark navy wool suit and a white blouse. I was complimented on this outfit, for in the drab years after the war it was difficult to dress well. Rudi looked stunning in his special suit. Everyone told us that we were a handsome couple. The best man at our wedding was Anton. I sensed that he had serious doubts about our decision. Symbolically, we had no photographs of the occasion. I had a really good Leica camera, but I made a mistake and while loading the camera I exposed the film.

My new mother-in-law, Ilonka, was in her element and prepared a party to celebrate the occasion. It took place in her flat, there was delicious food, and unfortunately too much drink. At first things went well, we enjoyed the celebration, but as the afternoon turned into evening and night the party to celebrate our wedding became quite wild. Rudi flirted with Inge, and tried to kiss her. He got very drunk, and I loathed him when he was in such a state. I was pleased when it was all over, To divert my attention from Rudi's behaviour one of his friends, who had also escaped from Auschwitz, Czeszlaw Mordowicz, produced a pistol, and suggested I should learn how to use it. He took it apart and showed me how to reassemble it. I was not too impressed to have such a task on my wedding day. Still I excused these happenings as a manifestation of the pent up violence in Rudi and his friends after the long years in Auschwitz and then fighting as Partisans. I hoped that on our return to Prague everything would change for we would be a little further removed from our violent, unhappy past.

I longed to be back in Prague, in our little flat in Dejvice on our nice tree-lined road. My mother-in-law, Ilonka, helped us to finish furnishing it, and it was ready for us to move in. Our family life should have started, and as newly-weds we should have enjoyed it. But somehow neither of us knew how to go about it. To escape thinking of the problems in our relationship we concentrated on our professional life.

Shortly after getting married I wrote a letter to my cousin in

America, which he recently sent to me. It illustrates my loneliness, and how my marriage took second place in my life.
Here is a translation of the letter:

Prague, 18. V. 1949.

Dear Ďus,
I hope you do not mind that I am writing in Slovak, but I would find it difficult to express my thoughts in English. I am pleased that we resumed contact with each other, and hope that this time we will manage to maintain it. I do not like writing letters, but hope that I will improve. It is a real pity that the few of us who survived the Holocaust and are scattered all over the world, lost touch with each other. We should not allow this to happen.
It was good to hear that you like America and that you are happy there. I am convinced that one day I will come to America and find out for myself what it is like. Hopefully it will soon be possible. However to be honest, I wouldn't like to live there. As far as I am concerned I have chosen what I want to do with my life and the subject I want to follow: it is researching the physiology of the nervous system. Strictly speaking it is not a medical profession, for one does not deal with patients, but carries out experimental scientific work. I have been working for six months in a scientific Institute and receive a salary, although I have not yet obtained my medical degree. It is true that it is harder for me to study while having another job, but it is worth while for I am learning a lot. I am sorry that I can not write you more about my work, but you would probably be bored.
Ďus, you wrote that you cannot imagine me as a married person. Believe me I too find it strange. I cannot imagine you

as a married man either. To me it seems that not so long ago we were fishing together in Malženice using bent pins instead of fishhooks. Do you remember? When I think of it I feel so sad and nostalgic that those times are irretrievably lost. I am not sure whether you keep remembering those times, but for me it definitely was the most carefree and happiest time in my life. You know Ďus, it is because we have so many shared childhood experiences, and because later on our friendships and relationships can never match relationships founded on these childhood experiences that I feel it would be a great shame if we lost contact with each other. It is true that a letter is a poor substitute for personal contact, but it is better then nothing. In your letter you asked for wedding photographs. I am sorry but I can not comply with your request. Like you, I too have a Leica camera, but the film we used was damaged and we do not have a single wedding picture. Until now we have had no time to take some more photos. You have no idea how little time I have now. I work eight hours each day in the Institute, in addition I have to take care of our modest household, and then study for my final exams. Due to this lack of time I was unable to visit your stepbrother and stepmother (Karol and Jana), though I intend to see them this month and will let you know how they are. Now I wrote to you all about myself and I hope that you too will write to me in detail everything about yourself.

Millions of kisses

Gerta and Rudo

Chapter 5
The Beginning Of My Research Career

On my way to histology lectures which were given in the Anatomy building, I passed the Institute for Brain Research. It was housed in the Department of Biology of the Charles University. Ever since I had read the book by von Muralt about the transmission of signals by nerves I was fascinated by the nervous system. One afternoon in May 1949 after a histology lecture in the Department of Biology, I found myself in front of the gate of the Institute for Brain Research in the University Campus.

I mounted the few steps leading from the street to the entrance of the Institute and entered the building, walked ahead into a corridor, and was met by the unpleasant smells of formalin and other chemicals. Nevertheless, I carried on walking, until I came to a door that opened into a large room with benches, balances, and a few instruments that I had never seen before. There were three people in white coats in the room, and one of them came up to me. He was a youngish man, though then, everyone over 25 seemed old to me. He was quite small, had dark wavy hair that was beginning to recede and thin on the top. His very innocent blue eyes were looking straight at me from behind his glasses. I felt like running away, I really didn't know what to say, but the little man with the blue eyes looked straight at me and asked: 'Is there anything I can help you with?' I wasn't quite sure what I wanted, but this person was so friendly and so keen to help that I couldn't just walk out, which I felt like doing. 'I would like to do some research, for I am curious how the nervous system works,' I managed to say. This seemed to have pleased my host, whose name or identity I did not yet know. To overcome my embarrassment and to try to decrease the tension between us, he stretched out his hand and said: 'I am Ernest Gutmann, and I am a research worker here. Shall we go into my office and discuss what you would like to do?'

I was surprised to be taken seriously, and was completely taken by the friendly welcome by this Ernest Gutmann. I felt that this was my lucky day. Ernest led the way to a small office, the shelves were filled with books and journals, most of them in English, which I couldn't understand. The office had a homely atmosphere, it wasn't very tidy, there was a vase with flowers on the desk, and some sort of plant in the corner of the room. I introduced myself: 'I am Gerta Vrbová and I am a medical student in the 4th year of my studies. I read von Muralt's book, about transmission of signals in nerves, and I really would like to find out more about how the nervous system works.' Ernest seemed satisfied by this explanation, but took it all too literally. 'What research project were you thinking of undertaking?' he asked. This was a real challenge and since I had no idea what research was about, and knew even less what I wanted to do, I had to get out of this mess without looking too foolish. I asked: 'What are the possibilities of doing anything at all for someone like me, without any experience in research?' Ernest was so understanding and inspired so much trust that after a while I felt quite safe confessing to him that I had no idea what I wanted to do, or what research was about. 'We are quite limited here as to what research we can do,' Ernest confided. 'We have very little equipment and can do only very simple things. Why don't you come in when you can, meet the other researchers, talk to us and then decide what you would like to do. Then we will help you to get started.' I was delighted by this offer but couldn't see that talking to others would help me, so I asked whether I could start straight away. I was given a white laboratory coat and Ernest introduced me to the other two people who worked there. A tall, thin young man with untidy brown hair introduced himself: 'Ivan Rychlík', he said, and Ernest introduced me: 'this is Gerta Vrbová, and she would like to work with us. Ivan, could you spend some time and explain to her what you are doing?' Ivan told me that he was a biochemist and was studying how the distribution of water in different animal tissues is regulated. 'To study this, we need very simple equipment. Here in our laboratory we have a balance and an oven, and can record the weight of different tissue before and after it is dried, so with this simple method we can learn quite a lot about the way water is distributed in different tissue, and how this distribution is regulated.' Although this project was not exactly what I had in mind I liked Ivan, and thought I would be happy working with him. I talked to him for a bit longer and then returned to Ernest's office. Ernest looked up from the book he was reading and asked me what I had decided. 'I think I would like to work with Ivan.' This was how my research career and my friendship with Ernest Gutmann started.

Ernest made a very deep impression on me. He was different from any of the friends I knew from home, much more at ease with the world, probably because he was not around in central Europe during the Holocaust. He spent the Second World War in England

and escaped all the horrors of the Holocaust in Europe. Also, he had studied in Prague at the German University and grew up in the atmosphere of German Jewish Czech culture, so typical of Prague before the War. Indeed, he spoke Czech with a strong German accent, and that was quite strange for someone who, as I later learned, was such a great Czech patriot. I had never met anyone who was so generous and could share his knowledge and feelings so freely. He brought me Kafka's book, *The Trial,* to read, and then spent hours discussing various parts of the book with me. He also taught me that the place of work should be a place of enjoyment, and this as well as many other little things I picked up from Ernest helped me throughout my life when I had my own research group.

Most days during lunch time Ivan, Ernest and I rented a little rowing boat and rowed across the Vltava to a little Island (Císářský Ostrov) where we ate our sandwiches, sitting on the green grass watching the water flow by. These trips to the Island became a ritual, and we visited the Island in various combinations, either all three of us together or Ivan with Ernest, Ivan and me or Ernest and me. When I was alone with Ernest he often revealed to me his feelings, and I felt very flattered by his confidence. He told me that he was deeply in love with a young woman, in spite of the fact that he had a wife and three children. I was quite old fashioned, newly married and didn't quite understand how such a wonderful man could do such a thing, but I kept my reservations to myself and didn't ask questions.

Ernest must have sensed my problem, and once on a lovely sunny day when we were relaxed and lying quietly in the grass by the bank of the river on the Island he said to me: 'Falling in love is an event over which we have little control, it just happens like a thunderstorm or natural disaster. Have you read *Anna Karenina*?' I said 'Yes' and Ernest continued: 'you remember, she too had little control over her passion for Vronski. In the end it destroyed her, yet she could do nothing about it.' I listened to Ernest, and wished that such uncontrollable emotion would never get hold of me. Yet I realized that it must be quite exciting to submerge oneself in such passion. When later I read Nabokov's *Lolita* and his book, *Pnin*, and finally experienced for myself, an uncontrollable passion for another man, I always remembered that afternoon on the Island, where Ernest first revealed to me the destructive nature of these obsessive emotions. This idyllic spring and summer came to an end, and at the beginning of the next academic year, Ernest and I moved to a new Institute of Biology, while Ivan moved to an Institute of Chemistry. In this way our collaboration with Ivan ended.

In socialist Czechoslovakia the organisation of science and research was modelled on that of the Soviet Union, where research and educational teaching were separated. Following the example of the Soviet system, where scientific endeavour was concentrated in the Institutes of the Academy of the Soviet Union, the Czechoslovak Academy of Science was established together with a number of brand new Institutes of the Academy. Ernest Gutmann became Head of a division for muscle research in the Institute of Biology which was later to become the Institute of Physiology of the Czechoslovak Academy of Science. Apart from Gutmann's division there were two other divisions in the Institute of Biology. One was to investigate epilepsy and was headed by a young neurologist called Servit and the other division headed by

Křeček, was to study developmental biology. The Institutes were in Dejvice, an attractive suburb of Prague, and our Department moved there in the autumn of 1949. This was very convenient for me for our flat was only a short walk from the Institute. I had become passionately involved in my research, and could hardly think of anything else. My conversations concentrated on telling people about my work. It must have been terribly boring for everyone, so one evening when Rudi and I went for dinner with Inge, Eva and their boy friends Bubo and Anton, and I started to talk about my work, Inge got impatient with me and voiced the feelings of Rudi and my friends: 'We are not interested in your rats, but would like to know what you thought of the Ibsen play we saw yesterday.' I was taken aback, and had to admit that she was right. But that didn't stop me from thinking about my work all the time. In fact it drove me further away from my old friends and towards people who were interested in similar academic problems.

My friendship with my mentor Ernest Gutmann with whom I shared my scientific interests became very important for me. Ernest, who was quite a bit older then me, seemed to me to be very wise and experienced. He was enthusiastic about work, was always curious to find out how things worked, and his enthusiasm was contagious. As soon as we developed a hypothesis he wanted to check whether it could be confirmed or disproved. He grabbed a little bucket and went to the animal house to pick up some animals, usually white rats with red eyes, for the experiment he designed to test our ideas.

Soon several other young people joined our group, most of them still students and each of them seemed a very interesting person.

One of the first colleagues to join us was Radan Beránek. He too had finished his medical studies and after a few months of clinical work decided he wanted to do research, and joined Ernest Gutmann and me. Next person to join us was Pavel Hník, a newly qualified doctor interested in questions such as why muscles waste when disused. All four of us were deeply committed to our research. I spent endless hours at work, most evenings and every Saturday.

My lifestyle didn't do much good to my marriage, and to my relationship with Rudi, but I was so involved in my work that I didn't notice how it changed my life and priorities.

Graduation.

In spite of my commitment to research I did pass all the examinations of my medical course and enjoyed some of the clinical experience I was exposed to. For a while, I was in two minds as to whether to do full time research, or clinical practice, for I did like looking after patients. I was also very pleased that I had studied medicine, for it is a very special course where the student experiences so many different ways of learning, through reading books, through observation, through communication with other people, through doing one's own experiments and solving puzzles. Thus, when I passed all of my exams and finished my medical studies in 1950, I was satisfied with my choice.

The graduation ceremony took place in the middle of October, and Rudi's mother Ilonka insisted on having a real celebration in Prague. She was very proud that her daughter-in-law was now a fully fledged doctor. We also invited other family members.

Rudi's step-sister, Fanči, with her two sons Stefan and Jan came and my mother's brother, uncle Arnold from Slovakia also made the journey from Slovakia to Prague to be with us. The rest of my surviving family was unable to come, for they lived in Hungary and at the time it was impossible for them to get permission to travel, because the communist Hungarian government had clamped down on all travel out of Hungary.

My Graduation Ceremony, Prague 1950. *From left to right in the front row:* Ilonka, Myself, Rudi, Fanči and Aunt Terka. Behind: Bubo (Inge's husband) and Uncle Arnold.

The graduation ceremony took place in the Charles University, the Karolinum in the main Aula, a lovely large room. We students were all wearing black trousers or skirts and a white blouse or shirt. Our Professors had their hermelin-lined long gowns and fancy hats. It looked very grand, and quite ridiculous too. The Professors entered the assembly, and the rector of the University (Mukarovský) together with the Dean of the Medical School (Lukáš) called our names shook hands with us and handed us our degree certificate.

After the ceremony, we gathered outside, my husband Rudi, friends and family all formed a group. I received a large bouquet of flowers and we posed for photographs. My Uncle Arnold who had not seen me for at least five years was surprised that my hair, which was quite light and blonde when he last saw me in Bratislava, was now brown, and he said that now I looked like a really serious person. Rudi's mother Ilonka Néni was so proud, anyone who was watching our group and didn't know us, would have thought that it was her who had received the degree that day. When the tedious formalities were finished it was time to enjoy ourselves, and we went to celebrate the occasion in a very expensive restaurant nearby, where we spent more money on drink and food than we could afford. It was a happy occasion and somehow it marked the end of an important part of my life.

Rudi's degree ceremony in 1950: *From left to right:* Fanči's husband, Fanči, Rudi, Ilonka and I.

Chapter 6

Our Family Life

Meanwhile Rudi had also finished his studies in Organic Chemistry, and decided to become a biochemist. He was accepted to study for a PhD degree at the Institute of Biochemistry of the Academy of Sciences, and worked on the biochemistry of the brain. His supervisor Arnošt Kleinzeller, was an excellent biochemist. Rudi was receiving very good training and was becoming a very imaginative scientist. His laboratory was located very close to mine and was conveniently close to our flat. We spent most evenings together.

After work, on my way home I almost always went to buy some food, which was not easy, for food was difficult to get. On one particular occasion when I had finished work I decided to buy some special food for dinner. I joined a long queue outside a grocery shop where potatoes and some meat were apparently available. I was lucky, for when my turn came there were still some potatoes and some meat left for me to buy. I carried the shopping in a canvas bag, and walked home. I was looking forward to providing a nice meal for Rudi and myself, and then to relax together after our meal.

When I entered the flat with my shopping and plans for a lovely meal, the kitchen was full of dirty dishes, and Rudi was sitting in the sitting room reading, drinking vodka and looking miserable. I washed the dishes, and started to cook our meal, before going to see why Rudi was in such a bad mood. I didn't even have to ask, for Rudi started to tell me immediately that he had had a very bad time in the laboratory. 'They try to sabotage my work,' he complained. 'How do they do that?' I asked. 'You know what they did to me!' he answered, 'they hid all the scissors, so I couldn't cut the filter paper to the right size and do my experiment.' I stood there, perplexed and stared at Rudi, my disbelief clearly visible. 'Surely, someone just mislaid the scissors, nobody would hide them intentionally,' I uttered innocently. Rudi got really angry, and hurled abuse at me telling me that like the rest of his colleagues I too didn't believe him, and thought he was making it up. I went to the kitchen to finish cooking the meal. But our evening was spoiled, and my effort to have a specially romantic evening failed miserably. After several incidents like this I began to feel less inclined to spend much time trying to create a really warm home for us.

Rudi realized that I was trying to spend more and more time away from him and became increasingly possessive and jealous of me, yet we enjoyed many activities together. One of them was going to the theatre, and we went quite frequently. Tickets were cheap and could easily be obtained in the Department. One evening Rudi and I went to see a very good production of Chekhov's *Cherry Orchard*. We enjoyed the evening and the play we saw and were in a happy mood when we boarded a tram to go home. The conductor came to check our tickets, and I smiled at him. This provoked a terrible reaction from Rudi. He shouted at me in a loud voice that could be heard by everyone in the tram: 'you are flirting with the conductor, you slut.' I was left speechless, because nothing was further from my mind then seducing the conductor. But I was deeply offended.

Chapter 6

The more Rudi tried to restrain me the less inclined I felt to spend more time with him. I was very hurt by his lack of trust in me. And so Rudi and I were lost in a tangle of emotions. Rudi's paranoia, perhaps not surprising after what he had been through during the two years he spent in Auschwitz, made him see even the most trivial event as a sign of my infidelity, or disloyalty. There was no way I could convince him that although I did need 'space' to express myself and enjoy other peoples' friendship my loyalty to him was total. I could not imagine that in the not so distant future I will embark on a most dangerous mission that would change our lives, and separate me from Rudi for ever. Maybe Rudi did have some foreboding of these dramatic future developments.

And yet in spite of these manifestations of Rudi's distrust he did love me deeply. I realized that after I injured my shoulder. During the Christmas break in 1950, just after I obtained my medical degree, a group of us from the Institute went for a short skiing holiday in the Giant Mountains (Krknoše). Rudi refused to come with us, for he didn't like skiing, but he told me that he didn't mind if I joined the skiing party. We departed just after Christmas, and stayed in a hut in the mountains. In those days there were no ski lifts, and when one wanted to ski down hill, one first had to climb up the mountain, carrying the skis on one's shoulders. Our party consisted of five people, mostly members of the Institute. We had bad weather, lots of fog and poor visibility. Although I enjoyed the mountains, and exercise in the freezing cold, I didn't really have a good time, and I missed Rudi.

Still I didn't anticipate that this excursion would leave me disabled for life. On New Years' Eve we had a party to celebrate the arrival of the New Year and we went to sleep late. The next day we were leaving, skiing down to the railway station to take the train home. There was dense fog, and the visibility was very poor. I was not a good skier, and was scared in these weather conditions. I put my skis on outside the hut, but instead of following someone who knew the mountains, I just headed straight down. There was a precipice that I didn't notice in the fog, and I fell down about two metres. I knew immediately that something really bad had happened to me, for my right shoulder and arm hurt. My friends came to my rescue, established that I could stand up and only my right arm was damaged. I don't think anyone realized how badly hurt I was. My right arm was hanging limply from my shoulder, and each movement sent bursts of pain down my arm, hand and fingers. I was in agony.

Someone from our group put my arm into a sling, and slowly we set off on our way down the mountain. Although all of us were medical doctors, not one of us understood how dangerous it was for me to ski down with my injured arm. My shoulder was dislocated, and my arm should have been reset then and there to stop damaging my nerves. Alternatively, I ought to have been taken down the mountain on a stretcher where my arm would have been in a horizontal position. After a four hour descent, which I still don't know how I managed to accomplish, we arrived at the main resort and a regional hospital. The resident physicians anaesthetized me, replaced the dislocated humerus into its socket and put my arm into a brace. Unfortunately it was too late, by then my whole arm was paralysed, for my nerves (in the brachial plexus) were damaged by the injury and subsequent pull on the nerves during skiing down the mountain. Although my arm recovered to some extent, I never regained complete use of my hand.

Back home Rudi was waiting for me. We embraced and I told him what happened. I also reported that my arm was paralysed and it would either take a very long time to recover, or might not recover at all. Rudi was very gentle and comforted me: 'Don't worry, we will manage and you will be alright.' It felt wonderful to be home, and knowing that Rudi cared for me. Before we went to bed, Rudi filled up the bath tub with warm water, helped me to undress and to get into the bath supporting my injured arm and holding it out of the water. Then he produced a wooden ledge put it across the bath and placed my arm gently across it. From somewhere he was able to obtain a bar of lovely scented soap. At the time that was a real luxury. He gently soaped my body all over, then rinsed the soap off with a soft flannel, and helped me out of the bath. We went to bed, and made love with great tenderness.

I was incapacitated for a whole year, and spent the last three months of the year in Kladruby, a city near Prague that had a very modern rehabilitation institute, where my withered arm was nursed back to a functional useful extremity. During this time I was unable to work properly, but still did take part in the research the group was involved in, by attending staff meetings, reading, and writing essays. Health care in Czechoslovakia at the time was excellent, and I was provided with all the treatment I needed without having to pay. Nevertheless, I needed a lot of support and help, and Rudi did do his very best to keep me well while I was at home, but as soon as I went to the rehabilitation Institute Rudi changed and suspected me of all sorts of betrayals, including having a lesbian relationship with one of the therapists. After about one year I recovered sufficiently to be able to plan my future with Rudi.

Ilonka, Rudi and I, Prague 1950.

Chapter 7

The Political Situation Deteriorates

While I was immersed in my personal problems and later research, the political situation in Czechoslovakia started to change, but not for the better. These changes began while we were still students. We were unaware of the importance of the events we witnessed in February 1948. In a carefully orchestrated political manoeuvring the Communist Party with Klement Gottwald (then chairman of the central committee of the Communist Party and Stalin's stooge) in charge, replaced the democratically elected government by a new government that consisted mainly of communist ministers.

The communist members of the government raised more and more claims which non-communist ministers could not accept and as a protest submitted their resignation hoping that the then President, Beneš, would not accept it and call a new election. Gottwald claimed that many of the members of the legally elected government were in the service of capitalists set to destroy our Socialist country. Therefore they had to be replaced by comrades faithful to the socialist principles of the constitution. To show that the 'masses' agreed with these changes, large demonstrations were orchestrated throughout the country arranged by members of the Communist Party including the trade unions. Factory workers and students, myself and my friends included, marched through the freezing cold streets of Prague, gathered in the city's Old Town Square, carrying banners that were already prepared by god knows who, demanding the abdication of the non-communist members of the government.

On that morning in February, when we turned up for our lectures, we were told that some members of the government were traitors, and wanted to 'sell' our country to the capitalist West, that let us down so badly during the Munich negotiations with Hitler. Militant communist colleagues were organizing demonstrations and sent us to protest against these traitors. Thus instead of listening to lectures, we found ourselves standing, in the freezing cold, in the Old Town Square under the watchful eyes of the statue of Jan Hus. We listened to speeches from our communist comrades telling us that it was necessary to stop the treacherous non-communist government ministers from leading us astray, away from Socialism and our alliance with our liberators, the Soviet Union. Maybe it was so cold that our brains didn't work propely, but we believed these lies.

Under pressure from the Soviet Union, Klement Gottwald had formed his new government from which he excluded all non-communist members of the previous government (apparently the traitors). Presented with this situation, and worried about a military intervention from the Soviet Union, the then President Eduard Beneš, who was terminally ill, accepted and appointed the newly formed un-elected Government. It was from then on that the unlawful Czechoslovak Communist Government started to rule the country with disastrous consequences. It was extraordinary that we students, as well as most intellectuals, did not understand what was happening, and indeed helped this abomination to come about. I spent many evenings at endless meetings of the local branch of the

Communist Party in shabby, badly lit rooms listening to speeches of various 'comrades' who informed us of the dangers that threatened our country from enemies of communism from capitalists abroad, who were set to destroy us. We were told to be vigilant and watch for enemies of socialism everywhere. On one occasion I asked what I should be looking for, and how would I recognize such enemies. I was reprimanded, for asking such questions, for these enemies were apparently undetectable.

And then shortly afterwards the paranoia really got going. Since the enemies were difficult to detect, the universities had to be 'cleansed' of all bourgeois elements, among whom the 'enemies' might be hiding. My party organization at the University asked me to participate in the work of a committee where, together with other undergraduate students, we were supposed to decide whether a professor was suitable to remain in his or her post and teach. I got into difficulties for refusing to participate, for I argued that I was not qualified to make such decisions. Yet many of my colleagues liked the power, and made decisions based on information about the background of the person rather then their professional qualifications. If someone's background was middle-class, which of course it was in most cases, and the views of the person did not support the present government, he or she would lose their job. In this way we, students, lost some of our best teachers.

And then the 'cleansing' reached the ranks of the students: all those who came from rich families or had parents who did not support the present government were to be excluded from universities and were not allowed to study. This too was decided by committees that consisted of very young inexperienced students. The academic qualifications of both university professors and students were completely ignored.

Although I did not take part in the work of these committees, I did not have enough courage to protest against their decisions. Fear was taking hold of us all. Fear of what? Betraying one's convictions? Admitting that we had been wrong and backed the wrong cause? I, and probably many others were frightened by what was taking place around us, yet we didn't want to have our illusions about communism shattered. Nevertheless, I lost my illusions quite unexpectedly. Strangely it was the most mandane and apparently insignificant observations that eroded my belief in socialism.

To give but a few examples: we students were told that in order to build socialism more quickly, and also to develop closer links with the working class we should spend our free time working at various construction projects in factories, or building sites. It was compulsory to go out and carry out manual labour. I was part of a group that went to a factory each weekend to unload bricks. When we arrived on a Sunday we were told by a representative of the factory, probably a working class lad, to move the bricks from one place in the yard to another place, and when we came to the same factory, the next Sunday, we were asked to put them back to the place from where we had originally moved them.

In spite of such completely useless activities, each student had a quota as to how many hours of manual work he or she had to do, and this shifting of bricks was necessary for us to obtain 'brownie points' and credit for building socialism and supporting the proletarian revolution.

For me personally the nonsense of it all culminated on a trip where I was encouraged to join a group of students to go to work in Hungary to help and construct a canal that would join the river Danube with the river Tisa. Rudi was exempt from these duties, because he had been a Partisan during the War, but I had to go. This was shortly after Rudi and I got married, during the summer vacation of 1949, when we planned to take our summer holiday. Our group of students arrived at a desolate place in the hottest part of the Hungarian plains, with no sight of either river. There were just a few barracks where we were accommodated. We slept on wooden bunk beds with straw mattresses, infested with fleas. The food consisted of either potato or cabbage soup, usually spiced with hot peppers, so it was almost inedible.

We were given spades and told to dig trenches that would then form part of the canal. We were not shown any plans, or anything that would suggest that we were on the right spot, but we set out to work, and dug a trench for about a week. Then we were told that a mistake had been made and we should fill in the trench we had dug. At that point my common sense prevailed and I left my student group and travelled to Budapest where I stayed with my family, met up with Rudi and spent the rest of the summer going swimming to various swimming pools. But I was to be punished for this hedonistic act of defiance.

On my return to Prague I was called to attend a meeting of my party group and I was cautioned that such antisocial behaviour could not be tolerated. I was threatened that I will be excluded from the Communist Party. This was very disconcerting, for the loss of party membership might lead to exclusion from university studies. It was at this point that I finally lost faith in my dream of a new, just society that I was helping to build. And yet, like ostriches, my colleagues at the Institute, our friends, Rudi and I buried our heads and did our best to ignore the terrible disintegration of our society. It culminated in the show trials in the 1950s that convicted 14 innocent, leading members of the Communist Party and members of the government, headed by the previous Secretary of the Communist Party, Rudolf Slánský, of treason. Eleven leading members of the Communist Party, mainly Jews, were condemned to death and almost instantly executed and cremated. Their ashes were scattered in an unknown place. The other three accused were sentenced to life imprisonmment. In addition to instilling an atmosphere of fear, this act of violence was also directed towards getting rid of Jews holding important positions in the government and encouraged anti-Semitism in all walks of life.

I am writing this part of my story early in the 21st century, and to remind myself of the political trials in 1951-52, I read some of the accounts of the trials. Looking back at my life under communism, I find it unbelievable that during those years I had not been fully aware of the atrocities perpetrated by the government and the denial of human rights to the accused who were completely innocent. And yet I must have known that it was happening. I wish I knew what intricate mechanisms our brain uses, to prevent us from being aware of certain events we would rather be ignorant about. These denials of knowledge must operate in totalitarian systems and make it easier for the authorities to carry out atrocities that are unacceptable. And yet, I remember that a few months after our daughter Helena was born I attended classes for postnatal exercises to get into shape. One morning in November 1952 I was sitting in a clinic waiting to be shown some of these exercises. The waiting was made unbearable by the noise of the loudspeaker broadcasting at full blast the confessions of the communists accused of treason. This time the accused was Otto Šling and it was his confession that was broadcast. He was one of the accused men in the 'Slánský trial' .

Like the others he recited the script given to him by the interrogators admitting that he was a traitor and spy who had handed secrets to the Field Brothers, accused of being American agents, with the intention of destroying socialism and harming our State. Interestingly, before his execution Šling declared in a letter to the President that he had never been a spy, but neither the public nor his family was told anything about the letter. This was just one of the many broadcasts where the confession to treason of our previously respected political leaders was made public, and it made me feel sick. It was obvious that some very unsavoury tricks had to be used to obtain these confessions. This time, I didn't hear the end of the confession, for I was called in and my instructions for the postnatal exercises started.

Yet, nobody protested. To illustrate the cowardice of ordinary people, including myself, a surprising total of 2,355 petitions from various party organizations and even schoolchildren were sent to the President, thanking him for his vigilance and demanding the most severe punishment for the accused, and that happened even before the accused were convicted in a court. Not a single protest was voiced to demand that the rights of the accused be respected. Such was the fear and cowardice that permeated our society, including myself and my friends. Somehow, to mitigate our feeling of guilt we immersed ourselves in ordinary problems of 'living' and allowed these to overshadow the terrifying political events around us. Arrests of intellectuals mainly of Jewish origin, were taking place in all walks of life, many people we knew were arrested and not heard of ever again, and yet all this was not enough to awaken us. There were rumours that these 'political prisoners' were sent to Jáchymov, in north west Bohemia, to work in the uranium mines.

We too faced restrictions that were completely unreasonable, We were not allowed to travel abroad to countries that belonged to the Western Alliance, and even travelling to countries in the Communist bloc was restricted. In fact ordinary people did not have a passport, and on the rare occasions that we were allowed to travel, we received a travel document that entitled us only to undertake a single trip. In our work too, we had to pay lip service to Russian science, whether or not it was relevant to our work. When we wrote a scientific paper about our work, it had to have some mention of the fact that we were following in the footsteps of various recognized Russian scientists, such as Ivan Petrovich Pavlov, or others.

Yet our situation as physiologists was not as bad as that of geneticists, who had to follow in the footsteps of Russian scientists supported by Stalin who forged their results, such as Lysenko and his colleagues, or, alternatively, sent to the

Gulag. Yet nothing was enough to give us courage to protest against these events that were happening to our country. The economic situation was dismal. Food was not freely available, and many items were rationed, even eight years after the end of the war. Accommodation was difficult to obtain, and basic consumer goods like cookers and refrigerators were unavailable. It was into this disturbed world that our daughter Helena was born on the 26th of May 1952, and her arrival was for Rudi and I, like a ray of sunshine in a dark house.

Rudi and I in Prague 1951.

Chapter 8
Helena and Zuza Are Born

Helena as a baby in 1952: with Me (*left*), Rudi (*centre*) and Ilonka (*right*).

Helena our first child.

In spite of the distressing political situation, and the clear signs that our country was heading into a very dark period, there were some positive aspects to our personal lives. After a long year when Rudi and I struggled to cope with my paralysed arm, my arm recovered, I regained almost full function, and Rudi and I decided that we are now ready to have a baby. Our relationship had improved, and we desperately wanted to start a family. Thus disregarding the political turmoil and the dangerous society we lived in, I became pregnant. It was the best thing that had happened to me since the war started. My body was busy creating a new person! Here I was engaged in the ultimate of creative activity.

Chapter 8

Even my involvement with my scientific work took second place. Rudi was nice and gentle to me and it was the happiest time we had together since we got married. I concentrated on the wellbeing of my growing baby and since my baby and I shared my body that included me. I prepared nutritious meals for us, went swimming, attended antenatal classes and went for regular checkups. I felt the development of an independent being inside me, with its own heartbeat, own movements and all the ingredients that will eventually make it into a new person, a mixture of Rudi and me. Now that I was carrying Rudi's and my child, my love for Rudi became more unconditional and I could tolerate better all his swings of mood.

Finally the time came to have my baby, and one day at the end of May 1952 I thought that I started labour. Even at this early age my baby was considerate; it let me have a good night's sleep and started to prepare to leave me in the morning at about 7 o'clock. I packed a few things into a small bag, and took the tram to the hospital where I was looked after during pregnancy. I was quite slim and didn't look very pregnant. The porter didn't believe me when I told him that I was in labour, and didn't want to admit me to the labour ward. He told me: 'People do not come on their own by tram to give birth to their baby. They usually have their husband with them, their own pillow, and a large suitcase.' I told him that my husband couldn't come, and persuaded him to call Dr. Brodski, my obstetrician who was taking care of me and was a good friend. Dr. Brodski came to the reception and made all the arrangements for me to be admitted to the labour ward.

When he examined me he confirmed that I had started labour. I was getting ready for a difficult time, but after having been admitted to the hospital my labour pains disappeared, and I thought that perhaps my baby wanted to stay with me a little longer. I spent all day on the ward, walking and watching other babies being delivered, but my contractions stopped. It was evening now, and Dr. Brodski decided that if my labour did not resume in the morning, I would have to go home. I was very disappointed, I so much wanted to see this new person that was inside me, and did not want to wait for it any more.

I was given a sleeping pill and went to sleep. At around seven in the morning I woke up and in spite of being doped from the sleeping pill my labour pains now were really strong. The midwife came, and half an hour later my baby was born. I was lucky that I had slept through most of the labour pains, and just woke up in time to complete the final push to let my baby out. When the baby was born, examined, wiped clean and wrapped in a shawl the midwife said: 'You have a lovely little girl,' and handed me the little bundle. I thought that my baby was the most beautiful infant I had ever seen, and I couldn't believe that she was all ours. Her face was not wrinkled; she had a small nose and thick black hair. The midwife, a corpulent, kind woman who was most proficient and conducted my labour with great skill, confirmed that our baby was indeed unusually handsome. Even my suspicion that she probably said this to everyone couldn't stop me from believing her. Rudi came to see us a few hours later.

The reason for him not being with me at such an important time was that he had to go out of Prague to pick up a refridgerator that his mother managed to acquire for our little flat. At the time, having a refrigerator was a real luxury, and we didn't want to miss the opportunity to acquire one. So the refrigerator took precedence to his being present at his daughter's birth, and he came as soon as he could.

When Rudi entered the ward I was impatient to share with him my joy and show him our baby. He was wearing a light raincoat, and hurried towards my bed. He kissed me and asked how I was feeling, but he needn't have asked, for I was beaming with happiness. The babies were kept in a separate room and we asked the midwife to bring ours into the ward. The midwife handed our little girl to Rudi, and he took her into his arms, and gave her a most glorious smile. 'I couldn't imagine a few years back that I could be so happy, but this new life that is part of us, has made it worth while to go through all the suffering I had to endure to survive Auschwitz.' We agreed to call our daughter Helena, first because she was truly beautiful and would grow to be as irresistible as Helen of Troy, and second it was Rudi's mother's name.

When Rudi left, the midwife came back and said: 'Let's see how your baby will take to your nipple.' My breasts felt heavy and my nipples painful, so I was not looking forward to having them nibbled, but the midwife insisted that it would help. So I held my daughter's head close to my breast. The baby was turning its head from side to side looking for the nipple, and finally I managed to put my swollen nipple into her mouth. Amazingly, she knew immediately what to do and vigorously started to suck. After a while, I changed sides and offered her my other breast. The midwife was delighted, and said: 'I bet you feel better, you have a very clever little girl, she didn't have to be encouraged, and knew immediately what to do. She will be a good eater.' The next day the midwife showed me how to change nappies, and how to bath the baby. After a few days in hospital when my doctor was satisfied that I had recovered and the midwife that I was fully trained to look after the baby I was discharged and sent home.

It was already the beginning of June when I returned with Helena from hospital into our small flat, and I was pleased that we had made all the preparations for our baby; we had a cot, a bath and a lovely new pram. A balance to check how much weight the baby gained was also part of the equipment we had installed . We had plenty of soft cotton nappies, little vests and a special wrap with an embroidered cover.

To celebrate Helena's arrival we had a big party to introduce our daughter to our friends who came and admired her. Indeed, she deserved the admiration for she was a model baby, very considerate, allowing us to sleep during the night, having big meals during each feeding and putting on weight. Breast feeding was a special pleasure, for this act still intimately connected our bodies. The first to arrive to the party was Inge and her husband Bubo. Inge was wearing a light blue dress that matched the colour of her eyes and looked very smart. She gave me a bunch of flowers, and asked whether she could hold the baby. When I agreed she picked Helena up, and her eyes lit up with delight. 'Isn't she lovely, so soft and cuddly, I wish I had a baby like that.' Helena was very serious and examined Inge. When she realized it was not me holding her she started to cry, and I had to take her quickly into my arms. Then the rest of my friends arrived, we had some snacks and some drinks, but Helena didn't like being the centre of attention and cried. However her love of eating overcame all distress, and as soon as I fed her, she calmed down and went to sleep, while we continued to enjoy ourselves.

During the next two weeks Helena was gaining weight rapidly and was becoming quite chubby and strong. She had a lovely smile she bestowed on me when she was happy and content after she had a burp after her meal.

There were some aspects of freedom we enjoyed in communist Czechoslovakia unknown at that time to women in the West. One of them was a long maternity leave. While in the West in 1952 women had no right to maternity leave, in communist Czechoslovakia women were entitled to a full four months. Conveniently, Helena was born in the spring and so we could spend the summer in the country.

When Helena was about six weeks old we decided to spend some time away from Prague. We rented a small house in the mountains (Jizerské Hory) north of Prague in a village called Albrechtice. A friend of Rudi's had a large car and agreed to drive us to Albrechtice. We had a roof-rack and were able to load all the things we thought we might need into the car. This took a very long time, and when we finished packing we started on our journey. Then after we turned the corner of our street I suddenly shouted: 'Stop, we have to return back home!' Rudi and his friend looked at me in amazement: 'Whatever for?' Rudi asked. My eyes were full of tears, as I explained: 'Can't you see, we left the baby in the flat.' Indeed, Helena was not in the car. We turned round and dashed back home and there she was, on our bed quite content, sucking her thumb. When she saw me, she stretched out her arms and smiled. I picked her up, felt the warmth of her body against mine and the soft skin of her cheek touching my face. Clutching her in my arms I ran down towards the car which was waiting for us outside the house. After this, our journey to Albrechtice was quite uneventful.

The little house we rented was cozy, and there was a large garden we could use. There were lush meadows around us and hills covered with trees. A stony path led from our house to a lake (Splav na Bílé Desné), where we could go for a short swim, while Helena slept either in the pram, or on a blanket we spread out for her in the shade. The air was clear and unpolluted so that the ultraviolet radiation from the sun was very strong. Indeed it was so powerful that it bleached all the stubborn stains from the soiled nappies when we spread them on the grass while they were still wet. They turned a brilliant white, by the time they dried. After two weeks Rudi, who had no paternity leave had to go back to work but I spent six wonderful weeks in Albrechtice with my daughter enjoying the mountains and unspoiled countryside. I was determined to return each summer, for I loved it there. Finally, the summer ended and Helena and I too had to return home to Prague.

I was convinced that our baby needed a lot of fresh air, so in addition to taking long walks in the parks of Prague with Helena in the pram, I put the baby in her cot under the open window in our flat. A lady from the flat opposite to ours spotted Helena, lying there contentedly under the window, and one day when I was walking home with Helena in the pram she stopped me and asked whether she could pick her up and give her a cuddle. The lady was in her early thirties, had blonde hair and a gentle face. She picked the baby up with loving care, and tenderness, and from that moment on, I saw that a love affair developed between the two of them. After this first encounter she came often to our flat to play

Tetinka and her husband, 1952.

with Helena and we called her Tetinka (Auntie). Thus our Helena found herself a nanny. Tetinka had her own two children, a girl of ten and a boy of twelve, and they accepted Helena as a member of their family. Thus, when after four months of maternity leave, I returned to work, our 'Tetinka' who was charmed by Helena's sweet personality took care of her while I was at work, which often included Saturday mornings.

Zuzka our second daughter.

Helena, was so delightful and gave us so much pleasure that we

Helenka, Rudi and I in 1953.

thought we would like another child. In spite of the fact that Rudi and I did not get on well or maybe because of it, I badly wanted a second child. Naïvely, I hoped that this would make us into a more united complete family, and that the difficulties between Rudi and I would disappear with the arrival of a new baby. And so on the 3rd of May 1954, just before Helena's second birthday, my second daughter was born in the same maternity ward and helped into the world by the same midwife as Helena had. She too was a lovely little girl, but looked much more fragile then Helena. She had delicate white skin and a small amount of fluffy blonde hair. We called her Zuzka, just because we thought the name suited her.

Rudi and Helena visited us in hospital and Helena asked whether she could hold the baby in her arms. She carefully lifted the baby out of the cot and held her expertly in her little arms, a big smile on her face. The bonding between the two sisters had started. Unfortunately, just before we were due to come home, Helena fell ill with whooping cough. She was not allowed to have contact with the new baby for whooping cough can be a deadly disease for newborn babies. We had to separate our two daughters and Helena

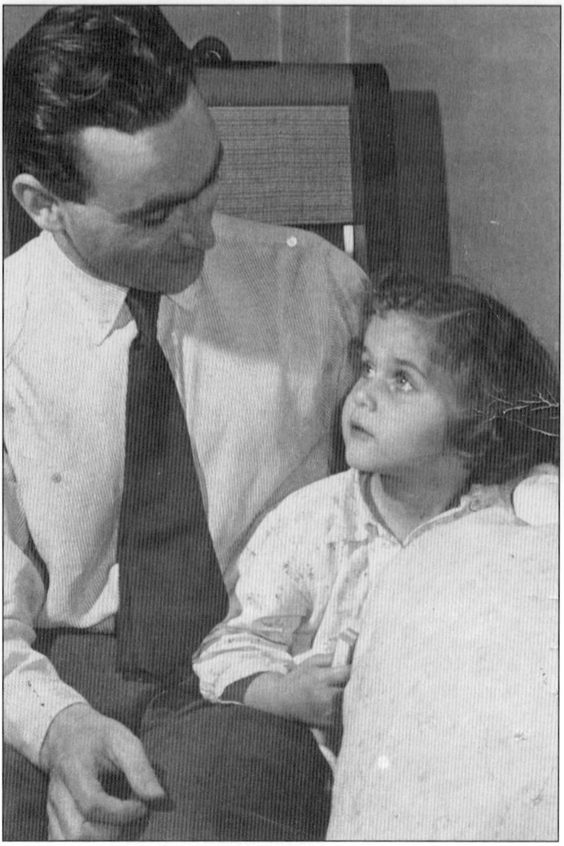

Rudi and Helenka in 1954.

had to stay away from our flat in Tetinka's house. So Helena's pleasure and happiness of having a baby sister was marred by her illness. We re-arranged our flat to accommodate the new baby. We got a small bed for Helena and Zuzka inherited the cot. While Helena was ill we were very anxious and worried about our new baby, for whooping cough was such a dangerous disease. But Zuza did not contract whooping cough and was a healthy baby. She was however not such a greedy eater as her older sister was, and had to have a lot of encouragement to eat. Because of Helena's illness we had no party to celebrate Zuzka's arrival, and introduced her to our friends gradually.

Soon Helena recovered from her illness, and when she finally could spend time with her baby sister she loved it. She enjoyed helping me to change the nappies, and to bath her in what used to be her baby bath. Although only just over two years old Helena was very talkative, she was making up stories that she was telling us. Helena also liked to sing songs that Tetinka taught her and knew a lot of them by heart. One evening after I put the children to bed I heard singing from their room. I opened the door quietly, and saw Helena standing by Zuza's cot and singing a lullaby to her.

In July the whole family went again to Albrechtice, to the same cottage we had rented the previous year. We also took a friend of Helena's with us, little Olga. She was the daughter of my friend and colleague, with whom I shared an office at work. The mountain nearest to our house was called Špičák, and in July and August there were wild raspberries growing in the woods. Helena and Olga were old enough to come with us to pick wild raspberries that grew in the forest while Zuza had to be carried. It was a very happy summer, but it was over too fast, and even before I could get used to having two lovely daughters I had to return to work. While I was working Tetinka took care of both my little girls, but I think, Helena was always closer to her heart then Zuzka. I was very lucky that Helena could talk well, and was observant and articulate,

Rudi and Zuzka in 1955.

for even at this early age, she was always able to tell me how she and Zuzka spent their time while I was working. I was therefore never worried about not knowing what was happening while I was at work. Even in 1954 almost ten years after the war, there was still a shortage of food, and therefore children were given extra rations. Our two daughters got two eggs a week each in addition to some

sugar and butter. I treasured these supplements. Then one morning I wanted to use some of the eggs to prepare pancakes for the children, but to my amazement I discovered that the eggs had disappeared. When I looked into it I discovered that Rudi had eaten them without asking me. Somehow, this upset me out of all proportions and I felt not only very hurt by Rudi but also antagonistic to him. Looking back at this incident now, it seems petty but at the time it seemed very serious. Also, perhaps I didn't realize that, as in Auschwitz, Rudi thought that food should be consumed straight away and not left hanging about.

Divorce.

Rudi had a very strange idea about parenting. He did love both our children, Helena and Zuzka, but somehow they had to fit into his life. He quite frequently went out drinking with his friends at night, and came home late when all of us were asleep. Instead of entering the flat so as not to disturb us, he would open the door to our bedroom, wake up both the children and play with them in the middle of the night for an hour or so. When he got bored, it was up to me to get them back to sleep. Next morning the children were tired and in a bad mood. I tried to talk to him about this, but he didn't see that there was anything wrong with his behavior. Our relationship again deteriorated, and we found it more and more difficult to live together. I felt that we were not providing a pleasant environment for our young children. Finally I wanted a divorce, but Rudi resisted the idea, though he did nothing to make life together better. Divorcing Rudi was a hard decision, I still felt attached to him, though I am not sure that I loved him. Our two daughters loved him and needed both of us but our home environment was tense and unhappy. To avoid arguments and clashes, we tried to live separately in our little flat. The children slept with me in the bedroom and the sitting room was used by Rudi. The final straw that made me decide that I wanted a divorce was the night when I heard the door of our flat open, and Rudi with his girlfriend enter. They were both drunk, and very noisy. I could hear them making love on the sofa of the sitting room. The children were also awake, because of the noise made by Rudi and his lover. Such incidents together with the incongruous jealousy and mistrust that Rudi had of my friends finally convinced me that I had only one option: divorce. After protracted arguments, and unsuccessful attempts to change our behaviour towards each other Rudi agreed to a divorce, though I had to pay all the legal costs, leave the flat to Rudi and find another flat for myself and the children. That proved to be a very difficult task because at the time there was a desperate shortage of accommodation. To help me with my divorce I found a solicitor in the telephone directory called Svoboda, which means freedom, so I chose him, for I felt that separating from Rudi would bring me a bit more freedom.

Chapter 9

Our Research Team Develops

Hanka and I in the laboratory 1954.

Back at work our group developed, and I became more and more absorbed in my research. We were all longing to meet colleagues from abroad, and so when I was chosen to go to Paris to present a paper in French at a meeting of the French Physiological Society I was beside myself with joy. Over the previous two years our group at the Institute of Physiology had grown. Many new people joined it, and by now, in 1952, we had a set of young people working together. Although all of us were working on the same problem—how nerves and muscles interact with each other—each of us had a different expertise, training and background, and therefore each individual was able to tackle the work using a different method. Some of my colleagues were biochemists, some physiologists, others histologists or engineers, and some of us had a medical degree. Ernest Gutmann, Arnošt, as we called him, was leading and coordinating our research. He had very advanced views and believed that a multidisciplinary approach would have a better chance of solving the problems we were working on.

Every Saturday morning the research members of our group met in the Institute to participate in a 'Journal Club'. Ernest Gutmann organized these meetings and they served two purposes: firstly, to make sure that all of us were familiar with the published data all over the world in our field. Secondly, to learn how to present data and discuss it. The seminars were held in a small room, with a table in the middle surrounded by chairs. Sitting around the table

Ernest Gutmann *circa* 1970.

and drinking tea during these meetings provided an informal atmosphere, and helped us to relax.

These meetings kept us informed about problems related to our work that were published in international journals and helped us to overcome the isolation and rather provincial outlook of scientific work in our country. Becoming familiar with publications in international scientific journals and the scientific ideas that other scientists were tackling was, for us, like looking through a window into the world. Each Saturday one of us had to give a talk that summarized recently published data relevant to our work, and one Saturday morning it was my turn.

I was very nervous for I had to give a presentation on a series of papers that dealt with control of movement and how the cerebral cortex is involved in this control. The papers were in English, and I had some difficulties understanding not only the science, but also the language. I spent hours preparing my presentation. I had help from Ernest Gutmann particularly in understanding the language, and I made careful notes of our discussions. On that particular Saturday I was surprised to find that once I started my talk it was quite easy to give a concise summary of the published results. I didn't even need the notes, I seemed to remember most results published in the papers that were relevant to our work. When I had finished, there was time for questions, and my colleagues contributed to a lively discussion. I was delighted, for it was clear that my presentation was successful and my colleagues understood what was in the papers I summarized, and also managed to pick out some interesting points in the work. Afterwards, my colleagues praised me and told me that I had given a stimulating talk. Even Beránek, who was the most critical of all my colleagues and seldom praised anyone, was enthusiastic, and said 'Well done, Gerta, that was a very good summary you presented.' Usually, after discussing other peoples' papers we talked about our own work, and discussed how best to approach the problem with the limited resources we had available. We also tried to find out from the literature which other scientists abroad had similar interests to ours, and wrote to them. We were of course encouraged to make contact with Russian scientists, and the Czechoslovak Academy of Sciences supported any possible collaboration with Russian scientists. Little did we know about the oppression and pressures our Russian colleagues had to endure. As well as increasing the number of colleagues working together in Ernest Gutmann's group we managed to get funding to buy some modern equipment. One day we acquired a new oscilloscope (to measure changes of electrical events in nerves and muscles).

We decided that this called for a celebration. My colleague Radan Beránek invited us to his home and we all brought some food and drink. Olga Hudlická bought some potato salad, Jiřina Zelená brought pastries, Radan Beránek supplied some beer, Anna Krejčová, our head technician, made a delicious soup, Hanka Karoušková prepared some rabbit paté.

Radan lived with his mother in a very large apartment in the centre of Prague. His father was an artist, and the walls of the flat were covered by what I believed to be beautiful paintings of Czech landscapes. We played jazz and other dance music on a battered record player. We all got drunk, but it was Ernest who was the most enthusiastic dancer. Unfortunately his dancing skill did not match his enthusiasm, and while dragging Anna along the dance floor he got too close to some of the paintings and knocked them off the wall. We realized that the party was getting out of hand, replaced the paintings stopped the music and went home. But the party fulfilled its purpose, and achieved even closer bonding between us, which grew stronger with time.

Hanka and Radan measuring electrical activity in muscle 1956.

We were publishing some of our results in a newly established Czech scientific journal, that was also read abroad and our work started to be known and appreciated by our colleagues outside Czechoslovakia and even some Western scientists showed interest in what we were doing. We developed links with some of them, discussed our work and regularly wrote to each other. Probably as a result of these communications we received an invitation, in March 1956, to present our work at the meeting of the French Physiological Society in Paris of that year. The talk had to be given in French, and my French was better then that of the rest of the members of our group. Therefore at a meeting of the members of our group it was decided that I should go to Paris to give a presentation summarizing our work.

Visit to Paris.

I was of course thrilled by this news. At last, I would meet colleagues whose work I knew from their publications but couldn't put a face to the people who had done the work. Also going to Paris seemed like a dream.

My children were now two and four years old. I thought that they could stay with Tetinka for one week, and Tetinka agreed to look after them while I was in Paris. I felt guilty about leaving them but it was impossible to get permission to take them with me. I prepared for my trip to Paris, discussing with Ernest and other colleagues how best to present our work. I was not worried about the science, but felt very diffident about my appearance, and worried about what I should wear and what hair do to have. I had never been to a western country, and somehow I imagined that everything must be different there and that I would stand out like a country bumpkin. I consulted my colleagues, and was told it would be fine if I will just be myself.

On the day of my departure I packed my small green canvas suitcase, I put my papers, presentation and slides to illustrate the results I was going to present into a smart leather briefcase, my passport and tickets into my handbag and left the house. I took the tram to Ruzyně Airport. The airport was a bleak grey concrete building, which resembled the nearby prison, and I felt uncomfortable right from the start. I met my colleague Franta Chytil, a biochemist who had also been invited to the Paris meeting. Our flight was a Sabena flight to Paris and after we had checked in we went through passport control. Shortly afterwards our flight was called and I was glad to board the airplane. I admired the blue upholstered comfortable seats, and the smartly dressed, very polite stewardesses. This certainly was a much more upmarket means of transport then our shabby trains with wooden benches. It was the first time I had been in an airplane; it was an exciting experience which gave me a foretaste of the luxury I would later see in Paris.

Just as I was settling down in my seat, and starting to enjoy the comfort, I heard my name called through the loudspeaker of the plane and I was asked to report to a member of the crew. I went to see a stewardess and she escorted me to the entrance of the plane. A young man in civilian clothes was standing just outside the door of the plane. He introduced himself as Pavel Voda, and said he is from the SNB (Statní Národní Bezpečnost) our Secret Service. He wanted to confirm who I was and asked: 'Are you Dr. Gerta Vrbová?' I was taken aback, and didn't understand what this stranger wanted. He then showed me his badge and repeated that he was from the police.'We received a report that you want to escape to the West, and plan to smuggle your children out as well,' the young policeman said to me. I was completely baffled. I was also angry. How can anyone do this to me, to spoil my first dream trip? The policeman, who was a very gentle looking young man with short blonde hair and very blue eyes, saw how upset I was and tried to comfort me. He said, 'If you can prove that you have made appropriate arrangements for the children to be looked after during your absence then there will be no problem, and you can travel.' 'But surely that will take time and I will miss the plane?' was my reply. 'Don't worry, we can delay the departure of the plane until we sort this out,' the young man reassured me. Together we went down the steps and into the main airport building. My policeman headed straight away to the office of the airport authorities to arrange for the plane to be kept waiting. 'You just wait here for me,' he said. There was nothing else I could do, so I just sat down and waited. My policeman was back in no time, and said cheerfully: 'The departure of your plane is halted until I give them clearance to leave, with or without you on board. Now let us go and find the person who is looking after the children. I will have to talk to her.'

He had a car and we drove to Tetinka's house. Tetinka and the children were surprised to see me return with a stranger. The policeman politely asked Tetinka to speak to him alone. When the interview with her finished, he told me: 'Get quickly back into the car, I will see you to the airport and put you on the plane. It is quite clear you told the truth and have no intention of leaving for good or abducting the children.' I asked: 'But who reported me, who told you that I wanted to leave?' His answer was shattering: 'Your former husband.' Nevertheless, I was amazed and comforted by the decency of the policeman, and couldn't believe my luck. I was quickly checked in again, put on the plane which was now, to the relief of all passengers, allowed to take off. I must have been quite unpopular with the other passengers for the delay I caused.

Exhausted by this experience I slumped into the seat next to my colleague Franta Chytil. I was still completely dazed from my recent experience and shattered by the realization that Rudi had denounced me, but gradually I relaxed and started to enjoy my very first trip on an airplane. It all seemed so incredibly luxurious, the smart stewardesses, the drinks and food on board, which tasted delicious, but above all the prospect of seeing Paris delighted me.

We arrived to Paris late afternoon and took the coach to the centre of the city. The Czechoslovak Embassy in Paris had booked our rooms in a most luxurious five star hotel, The George V, in Avenue George V. It was government policy in those early days of communism, when very few citizens were allowed to travel that anyone from Czechoslovakia should represent the country and impress our colleagues by the generosity of communist Czechoslovakia towards their artists or scientists. So there we were, stunned by the luxury that surrounded us. Both my colleague and I felt completely out of place, and were determined to move to a cheaper, more modest place as soon as possible.

My colleague and I quickly changed, dashed out into the streets of Paris and headed towards the Moulin Rouge. I am not sure what we expected, but as an example of decadent western culture this was the most important thing we wanted to see. We managed to get tickets and sat through the performance, watching pretty girls with few clothes on and glitter on their nipples performing some dance on the stage. In fact I was bored stiff, and couldn't understand why I had wanted to see this. Back in the hotel I revised the talk I was to give at the meeting of the French Physiological

Society. I didn't unpack my few possessions, for we were determined to move away from this ridiculously expensive hotel.

Next morning we went to the Czechoslovak Embassy and told the cultural attaché that we would like to move to a more modest hotel. He advised us to look at some hotels around the Boulevard Saint Germaine, and indeed it was in a small hotel in a street with an attractive name of Rue des Beaux Arts that we settled on. We did all the things that typical tourists do; we went to the Louvre, and other art galleries, saw the sights of Paris, and were exhausted by the evening.

The real purpose of the trip, to make contact with French scientists, was in fact more interesting then the sightseeing. On the second day of our stay I met western scientists for the first time. The meeting of the French Physiological Society was held at the Sorbonne University. I went to the registration desk, picked up the printed program of the meeting and discovered that my talk was scheduled for the next day. While studying the program a tall young Frenchman introduced himself: 'I am Yves Laporte,' he said 'I am interested in the Abstract describing your talk, and would like to know more about the work you and your colleagues do in Prague. We know hardly anything about what you are doing there, and it would be lovely to have more contact. Let's have a cup of coffee and talk.' We went to small coffee bar that my French colleague chose, sat down and talked. I explained how restricted our work was due to lack of equipment, and how we had to tailor our experiments according to available equipment. Yves said that in France things were better, but that he had just returned from the US and there scientists had everything they wished for. Then we both agreed that perhaps it isn't the best thing either, to have too much money, for it does not challenge ones' resourcefulness. When we returned to the meeting, Yves introduced me to some of his colleagues and I realized with great pleasure that all of us in the scientific community, no matter where we live or work, are really similar and that our passion to uncover tiny bits of nature's secrets is common to us all.

Back in the hotel, I worked again on my talk, revised it carefully and tried to memorise it. Next morning I went back to the meeting and with great trepidation managed to deliver my ten minute talk in French, to an audience of about 100 colleagues, whom I believed to be much cleverer then me. Several people asked questions about my work, and I was able to give quite informed, sensible replies. Afterwards during the interval, many of those who attended my talk came up to me to congratulate me on giving a really interesting talk. Some of my colleagues made useful suggestions, and some of them, particularly Yves Laporte, remained my friends. I realized during this meeting that people in the West were just as curious about us in the Communist bloc as we were about them. Finally next day, our last day in Paris, we reserved for shopping. The most fascinating glimpse of life in the West for me was in the big department stores that were selling exquisite luxury goods. The contrast with the shabby stores back in Prague was staggering, and I was astonished that such luxuries were freely available to everyone who could afford it. I walked along Boulevard Hausman and came to *Galleries Lafayette*. When I entered the building I was dazzled by the glass and steel dome, and charmed by the *Art Nouveau* staircase. Displayed on ten stories were all sorts of luxuries, and the goods were not even expensive. In the children's department a nice young woman about my age, asked what I was looking for. I was astonished how polite and nice she was, for in our shops in Prague, not only were all the goods drab, but the sales people were rude and never helpful. I said that I would like to bring something home for my two daughters aged four and two. With real interest the sales person asked about my daughters' hair and eye colour, and then showed me several dresses that she thought would be suitable for them. I bought two delightful dresses for my daughters in the children's department, and then proceeded to the ladies fashion coat section. There too I was helped by a woman who was working in the store and on her recommendation I chose a lilac mohair coat for myself. Finally, I bought a bottle of perfume for Tetinka who was looking after my children while I was enjoying Paris. I felt incredibly privileged and almost embarrassed returning home with such luxuries. For the first time ever, I felt deprived that we were unable to travel freely, and explore the world.

Homecoming.

My friend Hanka was waiting for me at the airport when I returned from Paris. She looked even more attractive than I remembered, and I was anxious to hear news about my children. She smiled, and said, 'I came just to let you know that all is well. I thought you might have worried about the children after what happened before you left. The man from the police who dealt with your case when you were leaving Prague came to see the children and Tetinka sent him to talk to me so I know what happened. But everyone is fine here, the children are well and they can't wait to see you.' After my luggage was cleared we took the tram to my flat in Dejvice, where Tetinka and my daughters were waiting for me. I opened my suitcase took out the two dresses, and said: 'I bought these for you, Helenka and Zuzka.' I wanted to see them wearing the new dresses straight away and helped the children to put them on. They looked really smashing. Tetinka commented that these were the prettiest dresses worn by the prettiest girls she had ever seen, and Hanka too was appreciative.

Tetinka made us all a cup of tea and then left to return to her home. Hanka recounted again in more detail how the Secret Service policeman who took me off the plane contacted her, and confirmed that the police had been alerted by my ex-husband that I was planning to abduct the children and use my trip to Paris to escape from Czechoslovakia. Now happily back home the whole incident seemed best forgotten. Hanka and I then arranged to meet the next day, which was a Sunday, on Petřín with her son Jakub and Helenka and Zuzka. When Hanka had left, I took out a book, *Peter and the Wolf* and read to my daughters.

The next day was warm and sunny and I dressed my daughters in the new dresses I had brought them from Paris. We were getting ready to go to Petřín to meet friends and have a picnic lunch there. I prepared some bread rolls filled with ham and cheese, grated some carrots and packed the food in a picnic basket. Then we took the tram and after a short walk reached the cable car that took us up the hill to Petřín. It was the first warm Sunday of the year, and the park in Petřín was very crowded. There was a small playground with some swings and slides, and that is where we met Hanka and her son, Jakub.

People were stopping to admire Helena and Zuza, for they looked fantastic in their new frilly dresses. Helena was shy, didn't like this admiration and was hiding behind my skirt, while Zuzka tried to impress her admirers. We spent quite a while at the playground, I was pushing the swing, and then watching both the children charging down the slide. Finally we got tired of the playground and tried to find a cozy place for our picnic. Hanka and Jakub joined us, we had a light red blanket that I spread out on the grass and we unpacked our rolls and ate them. I realized then that I had forgotten to bring any drinks, and we were quite thirsty. Fortunately there was a kiosk where they were selling drinks. Both the girls liked rasberry juice (malinovka), and Jakub wanted apple juice. I bought the drinks and was handed only one raspberry juice because the lady who served the drinks didn't understand that I had asked for two juices. I handed the drink to Zuza, and Helenka asked whether she could have a sip from Zuza's juice. Zuza agreed, but then when Helena returned the glass to her she thought that too much of the juice was missing. Maybe she didn't like her dress, or she was disturbed by my absence during the past week, but she got very angry and poured the juice all over her new dress. Hanka fetched Helena another drink, and I tried to get Zuza a new drink, but there was no way I could calm her down. To complete the job of ruining her dress, Zuza in her dress soaked in raspberry juice finally lay down in the mud formed by the spilt juice. She was completely wet and muddy, and I had to undress her, and wrap her up in the red blanket we used for sitting on the grass. This was the end of our outing, and we all went back home to our flat.

During the next few days, back at work I discussed the meeting in Paris with my colleagues and told them about the interest many of my French colleagues expressed about our work. Above all, I felt proud that my French colleagues thought that our work in Prague was exciting and innovative. This enthusiasm of our French colleagues, and their appreciation of our work inspired us to try and make contact with more colleagues from different countries and initiated the idea to organize an international meeting concerned with work of other scientists relevant to our work in Prague. However it was Ernest Gutmann who followed up the idea and worked hard to turn it into reality.

Our first international meeting in Prague.

It was quite a difficult and challenging task to organize an international meeting in Czechoslovakia in 1956, at the very height of the Cold War. The aftermath of the political trials in the early 1950s and the paranoia about the treacherous West, made it hard for us to get support for a conference that would include scientists from the West. And yet there was a great desire both on our side and on the side of colleagues from the West to exchange experiences and meet. Many of our colleagues from England and France, were members of an organization called *Science for Peace* which tried, through personal contacts and by providing help to colleagues in Eastern Europe, to arrange closer links between scientists who were divided by the Iron Curtain during the Cold War.

In our Institute we were fortunate that we had access to international scientific journals, and were informed about the progress made outside the Eastern Bloc. We therefore could select colleagues who worked on similar scientific problems to those that we were interested in and keep in touch with them. This was helped by the fact that several members of our group spoke excellent English and the head of our group, Ernest Gutmann had many international contacts, as he had worked in England as a scientist during the war. Thus, it was mainly thanks to Ernest that in 1956 we were able to organize a meeting to discuss the influence of nerves on muscle. We got permission to invite colleagues from France, England, and the USA in addition to those from Hungary, Poland, Russia and China.

International meeting, Prague. Sidney Hilton and Ernest Gutmann, in centre of the third row from the front of the lecture theatre.

To our surprise, most of the colleagues we invited accepted our invitation, even though we could offer them little financial support to attend the meeting. To compensate for this we managed to secure a beautiful venue for the conference—a delightful old monastery in Strahov near the Prague Castle. The government wanted to impress our foreign visitors by showing them that science was well supported in our communist country, and the Czech Academy of Sciences therefore provided us with various perks, such as allowing us to use their chauffeur driven vehicles to pick up our visitors from the airport, and for making it possible for us to organize some trips to show our visitors the beauty of our country.

My task was to fetch a distinguished Chinese (T.P. Feng) and a French (Jean Dreyfus) colleague from the airport and take them to their hotel. The following day the conference started, and we hoped that all our preparations would be successful and that the meeting will not only be interesting but also enjoyable. Some of the conference participants from England also brought their wives with them, and so we had to provide a 'social program' for them.

There were noticeable differences between my Russian colleagues to those from Western countries; our Russian colleagues were tense, shabbily dressed, rather subdued and not accompanied by their wives or husbands. Only when they had drunk some alcohol and became a little inebriated, did they relax a bit, and some of them had very strange habits. One large Russian physiologist loved beer, but before he drank it he put a lot of salt into it. This produced a small explosion, a lot of foam and a terrible mess. God knows how the beer tasted, but Ernest Gutmann was suitably impressed. Our colleagues from Britain and France were more relaxed, and easier to talk to. There was a particular person Sidney Hilton, who came from London, whom I found very attractive. He was curious about everything, our work, our lives, families and our culture. Another person that was eager to learn about how we lived was a French biochemist, Jean Dreyfus, who sympathized with our political system and wanted to learn more about how it worked. We spent many hours discussing the advantages and problems of living in the two different social systems, and I couldn't help feeling disadvantaged living under the communist system. It became clear that our working conditions were inferior to those of our colleagues from the West. While our Western colleagues had access to modern equipment and chemicals we were restricted to much more basic facilities and our work was constrained by shortages unknown to our western colleagues.

One evening after the meeting had finished, a few of us were sitting in small café just behind the Castle and felt particularly relaxed. From our Institute there was Olga Hudlická, Ernest Gutmann and me, and only two Western colleagues were with us, Dr. Dreyfus and Sidney Hilton. Dr. Dreyfus turned to me and asked: 'Why do you always start your papers by praising an established Russian scientist, even though what he has done has nothing to do with your work?' My friends told me that my face turned bright pink. I felt even worse than what I looked like, for how can I explain to these people, who were completely free to think and write what they wanted, that we were not. I pulled myself together and gave a dangerously honest answer: 'The leadership of the Academy demands that we should pay lip service to Soviet science, and since the funding of our Institute, and indeed our jobs depend on the people in charge of the Academy, we feel that this is a small price to pay for their support.' My colleagues and I felt deeply embarrassed, but at least we had given our friends from the West an honest answer. I then turned to my English colleague Sidney Hilton: 'What is it like in England? How do you get money for your work?' Sidney tried to explain: 'Some funding is available at Universities, but if you have a special project then you have to apply to the Medical Research

Council, which will get your application reviewed by experts and then decide whether or not to fund it. As you see our system also is not impartial, for whether or not you will get funded depends on the colleagues who may or may not like your work, and there is of course a lot of personal bias in these assessments.' The answer pleased me, for I felt that maybe the system in the West is not perfect either.

We took our guests back to the hotel, where Sidney's wife Beth was waiting for him. Her shiny black hair was cut short, and suited her attractive, quite exotic looking face. She was pregnant, but in spite of that moved gracefully. She was smartly dressed, her clothes simple and well cut. She told us that she had had a very good day, sightseeing and enjoyed her stay in Prague. We discussed the plan for the next day, when all the participants of the meeting were to be driven by coach first to a castle called Zvikov and then we planned to have a picnic near Orlík, a particularly attractive spot on the bank of river Vltava. Beth wasn't sure whether she would come, for she feared it might be too strenuous for her, but she insisted that Sidney should go with the rest of us. We left our guests in the hotel and went home. I was pleased, for it had been a long day and I was looking forward to see my children, who were with their baby minder, Tetinka. I picked them up, and we went to our little flat, where we had something to eat, played and went to bed.

The next morning the coach picked us up outside Strahov monastery and we went on our trip. Our first stop was Zvikov a spectacular Gothic Castle situated at the confluence of the Vltava and Otava rivers, and surrounded almost entirely by water. It has a spectacular arcaded gallery, and a chapel. We walked around the Castle, and the atmosphere had a deep influence on us. Sidney attached himself to me, and I enjoyed being near him. We walked together, and almost without noticing started to hold hands. I wasn't concerned that we were becoming attached to each other, for I knew that he would leave for England in two days time and I will probably never see him again. Yet on that day in Zvikov being with him and touching him felt very good.

It was a hot day and by lunch time, we were ready to cool down. On the way back to Prague we stopped by another castle, Orlík. It was on the river Vltava where a large dam was built and created a picturesque lake named after the castle Orlík. My friend Olga and I had our swimming costumes with us and thought that a swim would be very pleasant. After we had briefly toured Orlík castle, Olga suggested that we should go for a swim. This idea was taken up with great enthusiasm, but only Olga and I had brought a swimming costume, so the only way to allow our guests to enjoy a swim was to share the two swimming costumes. Conveniently only two of our guests wanted a swim: the Frenchman Dreyfus and the Englishman Sidney Hilton. Sidney was quick to book my swimming costume, and Dreyfus had Olga's. Olga and I went for a swim first, and it was wonderfully refreshing. The water was clear and cool, and after our exertion in the heat we felt thoroughly refreshed. We were sorry we could not splash about in the water together with the rest of the party, but there was nothing we could do. We got out of the water changed into our clothes and handed our wet swimming costumes to our visitors. Both Dreyfus and Hilton changed into our swimming costumes and looked quite ridiculous, which made everyone laugh, created an even more lighthearted atmosphere and a memorable trip. Somehow sharing my swimming costume with Sidney created a strange feeling of intimacy between the two of us. When everyone finished swimming we had our picnic lunch, and drove back to Prague in the coach. It was a wonderful day and it showed that no barricades erected by the Cold War can stop friendship and love.

Helenka in 1956.

Chapter 10

A Single Parent In A Communist Country

Helenka in Hungary in 1957.

Yet another move.

After the meeting our visitors went home and our life continued. For me personally it was a difficult time particularly because it was near to impossible to obtain alternative accommodation. Although we were now divorced, Rudi didn't want to move out of the flat we shared. Helena, Zuza and I moved into the bedroom, and Rudi occupied the sitting room. Our bedroom didn't have a separate entrance from the hall and we had to go through the sitting room.

Also to access the bathroom we needed to go through the sitting room. This situation may have been less awkward if Rudi didn't bring a succession of girl friends to stay overnight with him in the sitting room, while Helena, Zuza and I were trying to sleep in the bedroom we now shared. All this was emotionally damaging to us all, and I was determined to find another flat. But this was a very difficult task at that time in Czechoslovakia, for there was a serious shortage of accommodation in Prague. Flats were allotted to applicants by the local authorities and such allocations depended on a variety of factors. One condition was that any applicant needed to have accumulated at least 200 hours of manual labour on a building site to his or her credit. That would take a very long time for me to achieve, for I was able to work only on Sundays, and had to find someone who would look after the children while I was working on a building site. At one of the Saturday meetings of our group at the Institute I presented this problem to my colleagues, and asked for advice. Beránek found a simple solution: 'Why don't we help Gerta, we can go to a building site and get several hours of manual labour to our credit and then transfer it to Gerta.' This proposal was enthusiastically accepted, and indeed my colleagues spent four weekends working on a building site for my benefit. In this way I had the right number of hours of manual labour within one month, and a flat in the following two weeks.

The flat was very small, an entrance hall, kitchen and bedroom, but I was beside myself with joy because I would now be able to move out and start a new life with my daughters. It was quite a gigantic task to create a comfortable home for all three of us in this small space. I had wanted the children to have a separate room, where they could play and sleep without being disturbed, and the only space available was the kitchen. Thus the kitchen had to be transformed into a nice room for the children, and some cooking facilities had to be installed somewhere else. The only available space was the entrance hall, and it was there that I installed a little kitchenette. On closer inspection of the new flat's facilities other problems surfaced, the most important being the lack of hot water. A boiler had to be installed somewhere, probably in the bathroom. All these tasks were almost impossible to achieve, for there were no plumbers, or decorators available that could help in the foreseeable future. My friends could help me with some tasks, but I knew no one who could do the plumbing and installation of a hot water system.

Our Institute had a very advanced workshop, and people who worked there had contacts with many craftsmen and skilled workers. I went to consult some of the people in the workshop. After some searching, one of the workers there recommended a plumber who might help. I met the plumber, and explained my problem. 'I am terribly busy,' he said 'and the earliest I can help you is in three months.' That was a terrible blow, for I was desperate to move as soon as possible. To get further advice as to what to do, I consulted the person in the Institute who recommended the very busy plumber. He gave me this advice: 'He (the plumber) is an ice hockey fanatic, and if you could get him tickets for ice hockey matches, he will do anything for you.' This was wonderful news since my research was concerned with the question: how do muscles work? I was a member of the Sports Council of Czechoslovakia, and had access to tickets to all the ice hockey or football matches.

I got tickets to four ice hockey matches, and asked the plumber: 'If I give you these tickets, could you install the hot water and do all the work in the bathroom next week?' Miraculously he agreed, and I got the work done within one week. With the help of my friends I finished the rest of the work in the flat too during this time. I bought some furniture for our new home and so managed to move out from the flat where I endured so much pain and humiliation.

The new place was cheerful and cozy. There was a tall beige ceramic stove in the main room which doubled up as a sitting room, bedroom and study. The stove produced enough heat to keep the flat warm. Each morning I went to fetch coal from the cellar and made a fire. In the children's room we had a small electric heater, which kept their room warm. It was autumn now, and we were ready for the winter. I wanted enough space for the children to be able to play so I bought beds that folded neatly into a cupboard-like space when they were not used, and the underside of the beds provided a blackboard as well. We had a small square white table, with two chairs, and two chests of drawers for their clothes and toys. My friend Hanka came to inspect the flat. She had good taste and I wanted her advice. After she had a look around she said: 'Most of it is fine, but the floor tiles in the childrens' room look a bit drab. Perhaps we should cover them with linoleum.' I looked at the floor and agreed with Hanka. Then she continued: 'I know a place where they sell cut-offs very cheaply, we could go and get a piece. Let's measure the area.' I had a tape measure ready, and we measured the area of the floor, then we took a tram to the shop Hanka knew and chose a suitable piece of linoleum with a cheerful pattern. Together we hauled the linoleum to my flat on the tram and covered the old floor tiles with it. The room looked quite different and very cheerful, and when the children saw their room, they were really pleased and excited. So now the three of us were ready for a happy new life.

Visit to Hungary.

Our press and news on the radio provided us with very little and largely biased information about the political situation in our neighbouring countries. The sparse news that filtered through to us indicated that our neighbours were trying to become more independent of the Soviet Union. We heard from our Polish colleagues about the political changes in Poland, where Władisław Gomułka who became General Secretary of the Communist Party in the summer of 1956 managed to form a government that seemed to be implementing a more independent Polish style of communism that promised some degree of freedom to its citizens. And then in October 1956 rumours reached us that the Hungarian students and intellectuals had demonstrated against the influence of the Soviet Union on the Hungarian government. They wanted Hungary to become a neutral country outside the Warsaw Pact (the Warsaw Pact countries were forced to follow policies dictated by the Soviet Union). The new Hungarian Prime Minister, Imre Nagy, supported these demands, but was unsuccessful in achieving independence from the Soviet Union. There were massive demonstrations against the Soviet Union and these culminated in an armed uprising that attempted to achieve these goals and supported Imre Nagy's demands. Many of us in Czechoslovakia were hoping that Hungary would be able to achieve these changes. However, these hopes were shattered, when on the 4th of November 1956 Soviet tanks rolled into Budapest and most brutally suppressed any calls for freedom and independence. The part played by Czechoslovakia and Poland was a shameful reminder that nobody was prepared to stick their neck out to fight for freedom. All the Warsaw Pact countries, including Czechoslovakia, supported the invasion of a so-called sovereign country by foreign, that is, Russian troops. Indeed, other Warsaw Pact countries were prepared to send armed support to Hungary to help suppress the uprising. There were no protests raised in our country or in any other Warsaw Pact country against the violent Russian intervention. Neither was there any movement or individual effort to express sympathy for the freedom fighters in Hungary. It is with great embarrassment that I remember these times, for I, like most of my colleagues accepted the official explanations that excused my cowardly behaviour. The official view was that the uprising was an effort by fascist elements to destroy the way to Socialism in Hungary, and bring about the return of a fascist government. I did have my doubts and worried about the wellbeing of my family and many friends in Budapest. To see for myself, and get some idea as to what was going on, I decided to travel to Budapest with Helenka and Zuzka and visit my aunts and uncles. Christmas was approaching, and the time after Christmas seemed a good one for a visit. The children and I spent Christmas with Rudi's mother Ilonka in Bratislava, and Budapest was just a five hour train journey from Bratislava.

Thus shortly after Christmas 1956 we set off to visit Budapest. Our train arrived at the Nyugati (Western) station at around 4 o'clock in the afternoon, and my Aunt Manci (Manci Néni) was there to collect us. It was wonderful to see her, and so very comforting, for she looked well and happy, perhaps seeing us, particularly the children, cheered her up. Manci Néni's flat was only a short distance away from the station, and we took a tram to reach it. She still lived

From left to right: Helenka, Manci Néni, Uncle Andor, Zuzka and Me.

in a the same apartment block as before, built and owned by my mother's brother Uncle Arthur before the Second World War, but was now nationalized and owned by the state. However, both Uncle Arthur and Manci Néni had been allowed to stay in their separate flats. We arrived at Manci's flat, where tea was waiting for us. Manci's husband Andor was there, and I was pleased to see him, but was sad to discover that his eyesight had deteriorated so much that he could hardly see us. After finishing our tea, the children went to have a rest, and we adults started to talk. I was interested to know how the uprising affected ordinary people like my Aunt and her husband. Even before I asked any questions, Manci went to describe the events: 'It all started with the student demonstration in Petöfi Square, demanding freedom of speech. Then there was a confused period of various changes of government, and hopes that the Western powers would help to establish a neutral Hungary that was not aligned to the Soviet Union. During this time, some extremist groups were infiltrated by fascist elements and committed atrocities against people who worked for the communist regime, particularly members of the security services. Many individuals, against whom these elements had perhaps legitimate grievances were captured and hung from lamp-posts without any trial.' I could just picture it, and memories from the days during the war, when probably, the same people shot my friends into the Danube came flooding back into my mind. After all it was only just over ten years ago since these fascist elements had ruled the country and their representatives patrolled the streets and were free to murder any Jews. Most of these murderous individuals were never brought to justice. It is interesting and rather disconcerting that in contrast to Western Germany the Hungarians have never tried to come to terms with their fascist past and the people who perpetrated the atrocities carried out during this time were never called to justice.

When I watched the news about the Hungarian Uprising at home in Czechoslovakia I thought it was a popular movement that tried to achieve freedom for Hungary, but sitting in Manci Néni's flat memories of the days in 1944 and 1945 came flooding back, and I realized that the violence of those days could easily be rekindled, and that the majority of the people in Hungary were still attached to their fascist ideas. A popular uprising must have included a great number of fascist elements. 'What about the Russian invasion?' I asked. 'In some ways,' Manci said, 'it was a relief, though I had mixed feelings about it. It would have been better if the Hungarian people could have sorted this out among themselves, but I doubt whether that would have been possible. If the Russians hadn't come, we would have ended up with another fascist Hungary, since many of the people who participated in the so called 'popular movement' were people who ruled Hungary during fascism.'

At this point the children came into the room. They seemed happy and I admired the fact that they had adjusted so fast to the new environment where they did not understand the language. Helena, who was very articulate, asked: 'Will I be able to learn Hungarian and understand what everyone is saying?' Manci Néni who could speak Czech, and understood what Helena was saying picked her up, sat her on her lap and said: 'Of course, but for now I will be your interpreter.' Manci wanted to spend as much time as possible with my daughters so that she could get to know them. 'Come into the kitchen,' she said, 'and help me to prepare dinner, while your mummy unpacks your things.' They were delighted with this proposal, and followed Manci into the kitchen.

I wanted to know how the political upheavals affected some of my scientific colleagues and young friends, and what their views of the situation was. I telephoned a good friend of mine, Ervin whose opinion I always valued, and we arranged to meet the next morning.

Later in the evening before putting the children to bed, we went to my Uncle Arthur's flat which was just one floor below Manci Néni's flat to meet him. He was now very old, and quite ill, but still alert and pleased to see us. He looked at Helena for a long time and then said with much affection, 'You look like your grandmother, Józsa, she was my favourite sister. Are you also so sweet-natured?'

But all this was said in very broken, unclear Slovak, and I had doubts whether Helena understood what he said, but I did, and I was moved to tears thinking of my mother and realizing how much she would have enjoyed her grandchildren. We didn't stay long, because my uncle got tired very soon of having small children making a noise, and in any case, we were also tired and ready for bed.

The next morning after breakfast Manci wanted to take the children to the market, where there were interesting things to see and buy and afterwards in the afternoon she had tickets for a puppet show. She was very anxious to spend the day with them to get to know them better. This gave me time to meet with Ervin, and find out what he thought of the situation.

Ervin came to pick me up in his chauffeur driven limousine. He was head of one of the major scientific Institutes of the Hungarian Academy of Sciences, and had a chauffeur driven car at his disposal, just one of the perks of the communist *nomenklatura* (privileged). I first met Ervin when he came to visit our Institute in Prague and I was asked to show him around because I was the only person in the Institue who spoke Hungarian. Since then I met Ervin whenever I visited Hungary and we developed a close friendship. Ervin knew where I lived for he had visited me at my Aunt's apartment many times during my previous visits to Hungary. When he arrived we hugged and kissed each other, and I was aware of the affection we felt for each other. Even in the middle of winter he seemed tanned, and his blue eyes were bright in his dark face. He was, I realized, very handsome. Helena and Zuza were still at home, and Ervin admired them, but could not speak Czech, so communication was difficult. Nevertheless, having seen my affectionate welcome, the children too gave him a big hug and kiss, but soon left with Manci. Alone with Ervin I didn't waste any more time and asked: 'Where can we go and talk?' He immediately understood that I wanted to talk in a place where we could not be overheard, and I was not sure whether Manci Néni's flat was bugged. Ervin suggested: 'Let's take the tram to the Vörösmarti Czukrázda, as you know it is a lovely patisserie, and the cakes are still good. The driver can take the car back to the Institute.' That sounded just right.

We settled in the rather splendid *Art Nouveau* patisserie, which was originally called *Gerbeaud*, but acquired the name *Vörösmarty* (a Hungarian poet) under the communist rule. I went straight to the point: 'Ervin, you probably know what I would like to discuss with you. In essence I want to know what you, as a communist, think of the uprising and the way it was handled. What little I have seen of the city, its buildings have even more bullet holes than before, and people look even more miserable than I remember.' After a short pause, Ervin said, 'It is quite difficult to explain what I think. I am still too close to the wartime memories when the Hungarian fascists were murdering us Jews. During the uprising, the Hungarian people were murdering each other and us, Jews. Many members of the security services of the communist state were Jewish and were hung from lamp-posts without a trial, and many innocent people who were not members of any organisation were also unlawfully killed. There was complete chaos and the government could not keep law and order. Rioting and plundering was commonplace. I wish I could say that I supported the uprising, but I did not.' I was taken aback by this frank admission but I understood Ervin's feelings. Most Hungarian people actively supported the previous fascist government of Admiral Horthy, which formed an alliance with Hitler's Germany, and their cruelty was well known. It was only just over ten years since the end of the war and it is likely that a large proportion of those who took part in the uprising did so in order to depose a government imposed on Hungary because they had lost the war. It was a bad situation and I felt that the new 'order' they would have installed was nothing to look forward to. Ervin confirmed Manci's account when he continued: 'Look, Gerti, a lot more time is needed for the fascist ideology and views to change. As you know just over ten years passed since the same people that were now actively engaged in the uprising were shooting our Jewish friends into the frozen Danube, and signs of the same savage cruelty surfaced again now. It is a good thing that the uprising was squashed, but the manner in which it was achieved was bad. Had the law-abiding Hungarian citizens rather than the Russian tanks taken over the country, it would have been much better. Nobody likes foreign soldiers in their homeland, and the fact that the uprising was put down by foreign troops makes the people who took part in it look like heroes, rather than rabble who wanted to bring back fascism to Hungary.'

I must say I had mixed feelings about this, but the memories of those days in 1944, when two of my best friends were shot into the Danube by Hungarian fascists made me agree with Ervin. I too had a deep mistrust in the Hungarian people and their record before and during the Second World War was not good. Moreover, unlike in West Germany, there was no attempt in Hungary to come to terms with their fascist past, their alliance with Hitler's

Germany and the appalling behaviour of the Hungarian army when they invaded the Soviet Union during the Second World War. Indeed there were rumours that the Hungarian ordinary soldiers when fighting in Russia were even more cruel to the civilian population than the Germans. Also, without the co-operation of the Hungarian fascist government the rapid deportation of 450,000 Hungarian Jews to their death in Auschwitz in the spring and summer of 1944 could not have been accomplished.

In between these deliberations we ordered cakes and coffee and enjoyed seeing each other. We then talked about personal things. Ervin wanted to know more about how the children were getting on, and I wondered about his personal life. Although we had known each other for over three years, Ervin never told me anything about himself, and talked only about his professional life and scientific interests. It was strange that on one hand I felt very close to him, almost loved him, and yet I knew hardly anything about his private life, girlfriends and plans for the future. All I knew was that when I was in Budapest he had all the time in the world for me and treated me like the closest and most loved woman in his life. To confirm this, he was already making plans and asked me whether I could come to the opera with him tomorrow evening. There was a double-bill of Bartók on: the one act opera *Kékszakállu Herceg várja (Bluebeard's Castle)* and the ballet, *Csodálatos Mandarin (The Miraculous Mandarin)*. Ervin said that it is a fabulous performance and he could get very good tickets. So how could I refuse?

When we had finished our coffee and cake, Ervin suggested that we take a walk along Andrási Út and he would show me the lamp-posts, outside the sinister building that was the headquarters of the much hated Hungarian state security department (ÁVO), from which some of the members of the secret police had been hung during the uprising. It seemed to me a bit gruesome, but curiosity took the better of me and made me agree. We walked past the building of the secret police and the famous lamp-posts. Fortunately no one was hanging from the lamp-posts just then, and I didn't want to let my imagination wonder and visualize the bodies on the lamp-posts.

It was time to go back to Manci's flat and find out what the children were up to. Like a true gentleman Ervin accompanied me to the house, we said goodbye and arranged to meet the next evening to go to the opera. Helena and Zuza were both back, and so was Manci. They were very happy, and said that they enjoyed the puppet theatre. I had interrupted a card game the three of them were playing, and was told to go to the kitchen and make a cup of tea. The next day we planned to go to the thermal bath in Buda, where there are hot outdoor pools all year round.

Manci had a delicious meal ready for us. From the open air market in Lehel Tér, just across Váci Út she managed to get some goose liver and cooked it for us. After dinner we went to bed, but I couldn't sleep, for I was thinking about the things Ervin told me, and old memories of wartime Budapest kept returning. I was very disturbed, but finally fell asleep. Next morning while Manci was preparing our breakfast she told me the story of my cousin Baby and her family, which highlighted the other side of Hungary's political situation and the brutality of the Communist Regime.

Chapter 10

Baby's story.

My cousin Baby and her family were no longer in Budapest. Baby's husband Imre, used to own a factory, and the family was wealthy. They were therefore considered to be enemies of the Communist State. Baby, her husband and their three children were taken from their luxury villa in Buda, expelled from Budapest and exiled to a small village where they were allotted a single room, with no heating, bathroom or indoor toilet. They were not allowed to take any of their possessions from their house, each person just had a single suitcase to carry their personal belongings in. In the village they were given no employment and the family had no income. Manci said that she and many other friends went to visit them and tried to help out, but the life of Baby and her family was really pitiful.

To me this just confirmed my mistrust in the communist system, not only was it inhuman, but wasteful of resources. It seemed crazy to send gifted enterprising people into forced exile where they could do nothing, when their talents were so badly needed to restore the country's shattered economy. Not only was I very sorry for Baby and her family, but I was also worried about the future of a country that was unable to utilize it's human resources. I didn't have time to go and visit Baby in her exile, and only years later when she and her family were in Los Angeles and I visited them there, did I hear from her an account of all the horrors of their situation and how bravely she had handled it. Baby remembered, 'In the village people started to respect me, and I made many friends, for I started to educate women about how to treat and bring up children. We had discussion groups, and I was impressed how even after a day of heavy work the women would come and talk about their problems and discuss how best to bring up their children. When I tried to advise them, and they thought I helped, they would always bring us something, some eggs, flour or even meat. The women were also kind to our children, and tried to help us as much as possible. So altogether, it was not an entirely negative experience.'

After we had our breakfast Manci had to go to work, so I had the children to myself. We packed our swimming costumes and we went to the Lukács baths (Lukács Fürdó). There were several pools with hot mineral waters and all three of us thoroughly enjoyed being able to splash about or swim in the pool with hot spring water outdoors in the middle of the winter. There were not many people in the bath, but some elderly men played chess at the side of the pool while sitting in the hot outdoor pool. Both my girls were very amused by this.

We left the Lukács Fürdó and walked up the hill to the castle, enjoyed the view from the Fisherman's Bastion (Halász Bástya) across the Danube where the Houses of Parliament looked magnificent. We went into Mátyás Church (Mátyás Templom) and the sun streamed through the stained glass windows to illuminate the inside of the church with just enough light to make it look perfect. Though the church was beautiful in this light, my daughters were hungry and we searched for a café. Finally, we settled in a cozy small patisserie (Ruszwurm) in a small street branching off the Szenthááromság Tér (Holy Trinity Square) not far from the church. After we consumed a hot chocolate and some cakes we felt happy and relaxed. Fortified by the food, we decided to walk back across the Chain Bridge (Lánc Híd). On the way down from the castle I noticed fresh bullet holes in many of the buildings we passed along the way. Thus Budapest had acquired new scars so very soon after the war. We arrived 'home' late afternoon and felt quite tired after the swim and walk, but we enjoyed our outing. The children were pleased to see Manci and she too wanted to spend time with them, while I had to get ready for my evening at the opera. Hungarian women dressed very smartly when they went to the theatre or opera, but I had no smart clothes with me. I finally decided to wear a black skirt and a white silk blouse, which looked acceptable to me, but Manci was skeptical about this outfit. She found somewhere among her things a white fur cape and made me wear it.

Soon Ervin appeared at the doorstep and we went downstairs where outside the house a chauffeur driven car was waiting for us to take us to the Opera House. The State Opera House is a magnificent neo-Renaissance building. It was built in 1875, and when you enter it you feel like being transported to a truly magical place. We had seats in a box reserved for privileged members of the communist society and their guests. As always when we were together Ervin was attentive and very courteous to me. The performance started with Bartók's ballet, *The Miraculous Mandarin*. It was the most dramatic and moving show I had ever seen, and I was completely carried away. After a brief interval, the second part of the program, *Bluebeard's Castle*, followed. This rather sinister opera about the impenetrability of man's mind fascinated me, for being with Ervin I felt like Judith with Bluebeard in his castle where all the doors were closed and I couldn't penetrate into the secrets behind them. Except perhaps, unlike Judith, I didn't ask questions.

After the performance Ervin's chauffeur-driven car appeared in front of the Opera House and drove us to my home at Manci Néni's house. Ervin and I said goodbye, kissed and arranged to meet at the Institute for Experimental Medicine where Ervin worked.

Ervin.

Ervin and I saw each other quite rarely, and I didn't know much about Ervin's personal life and his other relationships, I only knew that when I was in Budapest he behaved to me as though I was the only woman he was interested in. This for me was very flattering and enjoyable, but also confusing. I was not sure, whether he was in love with me, or wanted a more permanent relationship, and I found it impossible to discuss this with him. I liked him very much, enjoyed his intelligence, sense of humour, and his charm. Like me, he was Jewish, came from Debrecen and survived the war in a Hungarian work camp, but all his family perished in Auschwitz. Like me, after the war Ervin studied medicine and decided to become a clinical scientist. He became interested in endocrinology and particularly in the function of the suprarenal gland, since as he put it, this tiny organ alone is essential for survival.'

I first met Ervin when he came to Prague for a short visit to our Institute, and I took him around to show him the work of our group and our laboratories. He looked at me with his blue clear eyes as though I was a miracle, and I couldn't help but be affected by the way he always treated me.

Whenever I was in Budapest visiting my family Ervin and I met, but I didn't learn more about him with time than during his short visit in Prague. In Budapest he was appointed to be Head of the new and very prestigious Institute of Experimental Medicine (Kisérleti Orvostudomány Központi Intézet KOKI), and I believe he was a successful scientist and administrator. I often enquired about his private life, and he told me that he did not want any permanent relationship and he never wanted children. The trauma of losing his family made it hard for him to accept normal life, and he felt that he could not be responsible for fathering a child having lost all his family during the Holocaust. So, like in *Bluebeard's Castle,* all the doors of Ervin's mind were closed.

End of our stay.

We stayed in Hungary for only a few more days, and then returned home. I was pleased to leave Hungary, for in spite of the fact that Manci was my closest family, I always felt uneasy there and the memories of the many tragic events I experienced in Budapest during the war always caught up with me.

Helenka, Zuzka and I in Budapest 1957.

Chapter 11

An Englishman In My Life

Helena, Zuza and I enjoyed living in our very own flat. The children spent every second weekend at their father's flat where they had many of their toys and favourite books, but the new flat we had was their proper home, and I was proud that they liked it so much. Most of the weekends that they spent at home, their friends would come to our flat and play. I enjoyed my freedom, and delighted in the fact that I could now invite my friends to our flat without worrying that they would be insulted by Rudi. In these new conditions I was gradually recovering from the trauma of my marriage. I was very careful not to get involved in any new relationship, for the possibility of getting hurt again frightened me. Yet I felt lonely, and missed being with someone whom I could love and with whom I could share my life.

Skiing with Sidney.

In February 1957 my friend and colleague Olga invited Sidney Hilton, a physiologist from London, whom I already knew from his previous stay in Prague, to visit her and to help her to introduce a new method for measuring blood flow in muscles. Sidney accepted the invitation and arrived in Prague, bringing us all sorts of presents, some of which were quite inappropriate. He brought for Olga and me nylon knickers, which was a far too intimate present to be given to women he barely knew, and a little humiliating too. What sort of underwear if any at all did he imagine we were wearing? Olga had hidden her 'present' in a drawer in her desk in the department so that her husband would not see it. The presents for the children were better. Helena received a green jumper and Zuza a blue one.

I shared an office with Olga and when Sidney arrived to our office I wished he would take me in his arms and kiss me. The attraction I felt when we had first met had not diminished and I enjoyed not only his presence near me, but the slightest physical contact gave me great pleasure. We didn't talk much to each other, and could not express our attraction for we were never alone. Yet his presence, his calm gentleness deeply affected me and filled me with hope that one day I may get to know him better.

After Sidney had spent one week working in the laboratory, Olga took him skiing to the Giant Mountains (Krkonoše). Sidney had never skied before and was very much looking forward to the new experience. Thus Olga and Sidney took the coach to the mountains for a one week skiing holiday. I was a little sad that Sidney was no longer around. And then three days after they departed I got a telephone call from Olga. She said that she had to return home, and begged me to come and look after Sidney in the mountains for two more days. She explained that it would be difficult for Sidney to manage on his own without speaking any Czech. Although I was delighted with the prospect of being with Sidney again, I wasn't sure whether I would be able to come, but promised Olga to look into it. Next day I asked Tetinka whether she could take care of Helena and Zuza for the next two or three days so that I could help Olga out. Tetinka agreed to look after them while I was away. But I was worried about being alone with Sidney, for

I feared that I might get involved and fall in love. To lessen this danger I asked an old friend of mine Pavel Fábry, to accompany me. Pavel was pleased to be asked and said he could do with a short break. So the following day Pavel and I departed early in the morning and went to the hut Olga had rented in the Krkonoše Mountains where Sidney was waiting for us. The three of us shared a very spacious but rather barren room with four beds and no other furniture or decorations. There was however a very attractive white ceramic stove in the room that kept us pleasantly warm.

It was early afternoon when Pavel and I arrived so we still had time for some skiing. The weather was perfect and the snow crisp and easy to ski on. This was fortunate, for Sidney really found it difficult to control the skis. I was hoping that during the few days he had spent with Olga, he would have learned some basic skills such as snow ploughing and stopping on a gentle slope. However, he had no idea what to do, and apparently Olga's method of instructing him was not very satisfactory. Sidney said that after he had put his skis on Olga started off and said: 'Sidney follow me'. He desperately tried to do this, for he didn't want to get lost in the mountains he didn't know, but this didn't teach him any skills. To help Sidney a little, Pavel and I found a nursery slope where we tried to teach Sidney how to reduce speed when going downhill and stop when necessary. Sidney was quite athletic and well coordinated and learned quite fast. We all enjoyed the fresh air, sun and exercise, and it didn't matter that we didn't take long trips.

We had dinner, and went to bed pleasantly tired. I fell asleep straight away, but after a while I was woken up by feeling that someone was gently stroking my shoulder. When I opened my eyes and turned round, I saw Sidney lying next to me and caressing my body. I felt quite relaxed and liked this physical contact with Sidney. After a while of hugging and kissing we made love. We had to be very quiet for we didn't want to wake up my chaperone, Pavel. I enjoyed our lovemaking, for I could completely relax and not worry about any serious commitment. After all, Sidney was British, and there was no chance at all that we could develop a permanent relationship and that I would be engulfed again in a marriage. So both of us completely abandoned any inhibitions and just enjoyed each other's bodies without thinking about the future. It was wonderfully delicious.

Next day Pavel and I tried to perfect Sidney's skiing. It was a beautiful sunny day, the snow a perfect white, the branches of the green fir trees gently bent by the weight of the snow that covered them. We skied on a gently sloping path along an icy stream, and all was fine until we had to cross the stream on a narrow bridge. This was a real challenge for Sidney's newly acquired skiing skills and he nearly fell into the river. Although we enjoyed the day, Sidney and I looked forward to the night and a repeat of our last night's experience. My English was very poor, and Sidney's Czech non-existent, so verbal communication was nearly impossible, but we didn't need it, for our bodies did all the communication. After we went to bed, we waited until Pavel was asleep and then Sidney again came into my bed, and we spent the rest of the night loving each other. Our activities at night were a lot more enjoyable than the skiing, and we therefore decided to return to Prague where perhaps we could continue these activities during the day as well.

We returned to Prague to my flat, and since we were not due back until one or two days later, and the children were away with Tetinka we spent the time making love. Somehow our bodies responded perfectly to each other, and took over completely. We were both surprised by this explosion of sexual desire and passion. Still I believed that this was just a temporary infatuation with no chance to develop into a more permanent relationship. However, when Sidney departed back to England I felt suddenly very lonely, and realized that I desperately missed Sidney, and that perhaps what happened between us during these few short nights and days aroused feelings that were more serious than a transient infatuation.

Sidney Hilton

A few days after Sidney left I got the first of many letters that Sidney wrote to me. He told me that he had fallen in love with me and had never before felt the same way about anyone. Many letters followed this first letter and in these Sidney gave me a detailed account of his daily life so as to involve me in all his activities.

Sidney was married to Beth, had a step-daughter from Beth's first marriage and together they had a young baby daughter. However, shortly after he had returned from Prague he moved away from their home and rented a flat where he lived alone and, as he put it, with me in his thoughts. This made me feel guilty, but I was nevertheless pleased at the same time, because my yearning for Sidney and feeling of emptiness after he had left, matched the feelings that he described in his letters.

I hoped that with time the intensity of my feeling for Sidney would wane, but this didn't happen, perhaps because each day a passionate letter from Sidney arrived and rekindled my feelings for him. Winter turned into spring and I had to plan my summer holiday with the children. I wanted to take them somewhere near a lake, so that they could start learning how to swim, and I was hoping that Sidney could come and join us. I found a small apartment in a place called Doksy near a lake in a lovely romantic setting, and I rented it for a week in July. Sidney promised to come and I was delighted that we would spend time together.

Doksy.

In the middle of July I picked Sidney up from Ruzyně Airport and I was surprised how easy it was to resume our relationship. I felt as though we had never been separated. We embraced, and kissed, and we couldn't wait to be alone. We arrived home, the children were waiting for us with Tetinka, and Sidney proceeded to unpack his luggage. He brought some lovely presents for the children. Helena got a thick, pink patterned '*Marks and Spencer'* jumper and Zuza a pale blue one. Helena was very pleased and asked me to teach her how to say 'thank you' in English. When I told her, she went up to Sidney put her arms round his neck and whispered in his ear 'Thank you.' Zuza was not so keen to communicate with Sidney; she made it clear that she didn't want him around and that she considered him to be an intruder. Whenever he went out of the room she lent against the door and didn't want to let him in again. It was quite difficult for me to know what to do. Helena was a great help, she felt that it made me happy to have Sidney around and wanted to please both of us. She tried to persuade Zuza that it is best for all of us, to have Sidney around. I got a lovely necklace and matching ear rings from Sidney and Helena thought they looked great on me.

I had prepared dinner, but neither of us felt like eating. After dinner, we played a game with the children, I read them a story and they went to bed. Sidney and I were at last alone, and fell into each others arms. We couldn't wait to undress and our bodies took care of the rest. Next morning we packed and all four of us took a coach to Doksy to start our holiday.

Our little apartment in Doksy was lovely, the weather was good, the lake warm and we swam, walked, played with the children and enjoyed each other. We discovered a small patch of sand by the lake and each morning we packed our swim suits, buckets and spades and settled down there. It was there that Helena learned to swim, all by herself. She suddenly came out of the water, took me by the hand and said: 'Look mummy, I can swim without a rubber ring.' She let go of me, dashed into the water without her rubber ring and swam. I followed her and we both swam out together. I was very proud of my daughter, but told her not to go into the deep part of the lake without an adult. Helena then tried to teach Zuza how to swim. She showed her how to lie on the water and splash her legs and arms, but Zuza was too young, and soon gave up and continued to enjoy herself just splashing in the water for a bit and then coming out of the water and building sandcastles.

Sidney and I were lying in the sun sprawled out on a chequered blanket. I was watching the children and enjoying having my new man who was becoming a very important person in my life, next to me. I started to dream that perhaps with Sidney the children and I could become a 'complete family'. Yet I knew little about this man, and was trying to find out a little more about him, his family, his interests and previous relationships. But conversation was tiring because my English was very basic, and I found it difficult to understand everything Sidney told me. Still, using quite simple language I did learn that he came from a very conventional Jewish family and that he was always under pressure to perform well and achieve academic excellence. He had a younger brother, Peter, who was a mathematician and seemed to outshine him in his academic achievements. Sidney tried to compete with his brother all the time. Having never experienced such problems I found it difficult to imagine what it must have been like for Sidney to have to struggle in this way. It wasn't till much later that I understood how much this affected his personality and confidence. I was also told that his marriage was not very happy and that his wife had a drinking problem. But the account of his marriage may have just been presented to me so as to satisfy me and make me feel less guilty about getting involved with a married man. Still at the time lying blissfully next to the man I loved I wanted to believe this. We went to our little apartment in the evening, had something to eat, put the children to bed, fell in each others arms and made love.

This pattern was repeated each day, with little variation and by the end of the week we could hardly believe that our holiday was over and we had to return to Prague. We still had two days and nights in Prague, but time went by too quickly and we had to separate yet again, and nourish our love through passionate letters and hope that we would soon meet again.

Visiting England.

I was beginning to realize that my relationship with Sidney was serious and not a casual affair as I had initially planned. If we were to develop it further and make decisions about a shared future, it was important that I should see Sidney in England, and that I too should see the country where I might decide to live. Therefore by the end of the summer Sidney arranged an invitation for me to give a talk at the Physiological Society in London in November. Since such an invitation was a prestigious professional achievement, it was difficult for the Czechoslovak authorities to deny me permission to visit the UK, and so with lots of good will from my colleagues and a bit of luck I got the documents and exit visa that allowed me to visit England in November 1957.

In order to find out what England was like, and whether I could live there I needed to spend some time there and decided to stay for six weeks. This was a very long time for me to be away from the children, but Tetinka and my friends in Prague assured me that they would take good care of them while I was away. I felt that this temporary separation was important for all our lives, for I wanted to be sure that Sidney was the right man for me and England the right country for us.

So on a rainy day on November the 12th 1957, I landed at Heathrow Airport and was met by Sidney. He explained that he had rented a small furnished flat for me and that he would drive me there. I was very impressed that Sidney had his own car, for in those days none of my colleagues in Czechoslovakia owned a car. We drove to 'my' flat, which was on the Archway Road in North London. The flat consisted of a small kitchen-dining room and a bedroom. Sidney did some shopping and wanted to introduce me to some British novelties. We had some sprats, or *whiting* which Sidney fried in oil and then we ate the whole fish with the bones, but without the head. I think I didn't like it and was not very impressed, but it didn't really matter, for all I wanted was to be with Sidney.

The next morning my exploration of life in England started. The meeting where I was scheduled to give the talk was not till the weekend of the 13th of December, and that gave us some time to visit places and for me to talk to some scientists whose names I knew and admired from reading the literature. The first day Sidney wanted me to see the place where he worked and meet some of his colleagues. We went to the Institute of Medical Research, a very large and relatively modern building at Mill Hill, North London, among lots of open countryside. I met the Head of his Division, William Feldberg, who was a very famous pharmacologist and participated in the discovery of the chemical that transmitted the message from nerves to muscles—acetylcholine. I also met some of Sidney's colleagues. I was very flattered because Sidney introduced me to everyone as his fiancé. I had to prepare my talk and Sidney helped me to work it out. It was decided that I would have a rehearsal in front of all Sidney's colleagues at Mill Hill before presenting my work to the Physiological Society. The Physiological Society had very strict rules according to which the speaker was not allowed to read his or her talk, was given only ten minutes time and was allowed to show only four slides. To accomplish this in a language that I couldn't speak very well was very difficult, and the rehearsal was an essential part of my training. After having worked hard on my talk for two days and taking advantage of all the help Sidney gave me, I thought that I was ready for the rehearsal, and arrangements were made for me to give the talk to my colleagues at Mill Hill. On the day of this rehearsal I was nervous, but nothing prepared me for the ordeal I had to go through. A small lecture theatre was made available for me to give my talk. I handed my slides to the technician who operated the projector and then sat down to wait for my colleagues to come. About 12 people came and sat down. I went to the front of the theatre and was ready to start my talk. It was supposed to last ten minutes only. Someone had set the alarm clock, to make sure that my talk finished in ten minutes. I thought that my talk was good, I knew it by heart and didn't read it. I finished in ten minutes and had only four slides. After I finished I was told by almost all of my colleagues that my talk was awful, mainly because it was not aimed at capturing the attention of the audience and it was boring. I was given a lot of advice as to how to alter it and present it so as to make it interesting to everyone. Apparently giving a talk involves a lot of acting, and I would have never guessed that this was important. Nobody said anything positive about my performance, and I was so upset that to my great embarrassment I burst into tears. Sidney was very patient with me, took me by the arm and said that he will help me to get the talk right.

We went back to our little flat on Archway Road and both of us worked on my talk, for a repeat rehearsal on the next day. After a sleepless night Sidney and I went to the Institute at Mill Hill, and back to the lecture theatre where I had had my humiliating experience, the day before. I braced myself to face the same audience and gave my amended talk. This time I was a little more successful, but I still was told that I had to improve my performance, and was scheduled for another rehearsal after the weekend. I felt much better, and was grateful to my colleagues for spending so much time trying to help me and teach me how to give a good talk.

Sidney had to work, and I enjoyed exploring London on my own, but most of all I loved the evenings and nights which Sidney and I spent together. We planned a trip to the south coast over the weekend, and Sidney decided we should drive South, to Pevensey Bay and take a walk along the coast towards Eastbourne. On a Saturday morning we drove in Sidney's car towards Brighton and I could not conceal my excitement of going to be near the sea. As soon as we arrived to Pevensey Bay we hurried to the nearest beach. The sight surpassed all my expectations. I was completely bewitched by the sea. I had seen the Baltic Sea, but this was the first time I saw the Atlantic Ocean, or rather the English Channel. It was November, and very cold and windy. The waves seemed enormous to me as they stirred up the shingle on the beach. We were on a beach covered in shingle, and the noise of the stones constantly being moved about by the waves battering the coast, made a powerful impression on me. We found a pleasant bed and breakfast place and stayed over night. The next morning as we walked towards Eastbourne, we watched and listened to the sea and returned to London in the evening.

During the next few days I tried to visit some colleagues with whom I shared scientific interests, but I was quite tense and worried about my talk to the Physiological Society the following weekend.

Finally the meeting started, and it was held at the Institute of Neurology in Queen's Square, London. My talk was scheduled on the second day of the meeting, so I could spend the first day watching other colleagues and assessing how these meetings and discussions were proceeding. The lecture theatre was quite large and there were about 100 people listening to the presentations. I was impressed by the informal atmosphere and by the genuine interest of most people in the talks. The discussions were even more interesting than the presentations, and showed that most people listened carefully and thought deeply about the talks. I was also surprised that most of my colleagues did not take themselves too seriously and often jokes and anecdotes that were told during or after the talks lightened the atmosphere and made the meeting more enjoyable.

At last my turn came, and I gave my presentation in ten minutes sharp showing four slides. My colleagues seemed to have enjoyed my presentation; they asked many interesting questions, and I could answer them all. After the meeting several colleagues came up to me and congratulated me on my talk. It was wonderful to meet people I only knew from the literature and whose work I admired. After all, this was the *Golden Age* of British physiology and pharmacology and at this meeting I felt part of it. I learned a lot about how to approach scientific problems and think about my work. I also realized that in spite of our efforts back in Prague to be as well informed as possible we were quite provincial and had not the advantage of being part of a much more developed and advanced scientific community.

Chapter 12

Making The Final Decision

Rudi with Helenka and Zuzka in Prague, 1958.

Discussions with friends.

I returned home from England just before Christmas, in time to buy a Christmas tree, decorate it, wrap up presents, buy some food and invite some friends for Christmas. It was wonderful to be with my children, we had missed each other and I decided that never again would I leave them for such a long time.

When I came to Tetinka's flat to pick up my daughters both Helena and Zuza looked happy, and I felt just a little jealous that they didn't seem to have missed me more. Helena welcomed me with a big kiss, and said: 'Mummy, I have a present for you. Do you want me to give it to you for Christmas, or do you want it now?' I said that I couldn't wait till Christmas, and it had been my birthday while I was away, so could I have it as a birthday present? Helena presented me with a lovely drawing of a dragon. Zuza cuddled up to me and with a smile pulled out a little parcel from her pocket, which she gave me. When I unwrapped it I saw that it contained a clown made from plasticine. I felt really privileged to have such a wonderful welcome. Tetinka reported that the children were very well behaved, and were a great pleasure to look after. I gave her a hug, thanked her for everything and gave her the present I brought home. A lovely silk scarf. She tried it on, and it suited her perfectly for it emphasized the beauty of her golden hair. We said goodbye and went to our little flat. There were just the three of us, and it was very cozy with a fire burning in the ceramic stove, which kept us warm. It felt good to be back home.

Next day I bought a live carp to cook for Christmas Eve and put him in the water in the bath. The children admired him and I felt bad about having to kill him for our meal. Perhaps I should just keep to our Jewish traditions instead of getting involved in making a Christmas Eve dinner, Christian style. But I had already invited Hanka and Jakub for Christmas Eve, so I had to go through with sacrificing the beautiful fish. As it turned out we had a lovely Christmas with the children and friends. I didn't know that it was the last Christmas I would spend in my country.

After Christmas and New Year I went back to work. It was the beginning of 1958, but I had no forboding that in this year my life will change for ever. My colleagues were curious about my impressions of scientific life in England, and particularly about the meeting of the Physiological Society that I had attended in London. We arranged a special Saturday morning, when I reported on my experiences. I described the ordeal I had to go through before giving my paper, and when I finished Ernest Gutmann said: 'From now on we will adopt the same procedures in our group. Before anyone gives a paper to the Czechoslovak Physiological Society, he or she will have to have a rehearsal. This is very important, not only because of learning how to present the work, but also how to think about it concisely.' I was really pleased that my trip to England was not only personally successful, but that I also managed to 'import' something useful for my friends and colleagues. From then on we tried to follow the example of the meetings of the British Physiological Society when our Czechoslovak Physiological Society held its meetings.

But life was not that easy for Ernest Gutmann and our group, for the growing anti-Semitism affected us. We had constant meetings of the local branch of the Communist Party where our work was assessed by a committee of the Institute set up by the Communist Party, and its members were often failed scientists. The quality of the research was rarely taken into account. We had to show that our work was based on Russian physiology, and glorify the role of the Communist Party and Marxist-Leninist ideology. These meetings were extremely tedious, though very important, for financial support for our work depended on the outcome of the committee's decision. The fact that Ernest was Jewish and worked abroad during the war did not help. If the committee decided that we were too 'pro-western' in our work, we would get less financial support. Moreover, our group had a distinct disadvantage: there were too many Jews, and with the increasing anti-Semitism within the Communist Party that was a real problem. Indeed at a Party meeting of all the communists in the Institute a colleague, Olga Burešová said, 'Do you realize that in Dr. Gutmann's group more then half the members of staff are either Jewish or married to Jews? Perhaps he should consider this and dismiss some of them, and if not, this group should not be supported.' Fortunately, most of our other colleagues did not follow this suggestion, and we did not lose support for our research. But it left a bitter taste, to realize that so soon after the Holocaust we were again targetted, and that all our effort and hard work to build up good scientific institutions had not been appreciated. This anti-Semitic atmosphere in the country and Institute strengthened my resolve to try and leave and go somewhere where I would not be exposed to discrimination.

I needed to talk to my friends about my feelings towards Sidney, my misgivings about my country, and my intention to leave. My closest friend and the one whose opinion I valued most was my boss and colleague Ernest Gutmann. We arranged to have dinner in a small restaurant on the Malá Strana called U Zlaté Studně (At the Golden

Well), which had magnificent views over the city and the roofs of the houses in the old city. We sat by the window, the roofs were sprinkled with snow, and the atmosphere in the restaurant was very romantic. It made me feel sad that I might leave this lovely city and my friends. Ernest and I knew that we could not talk freely about my problems in a restaurant, for we could be overheard, and our meeting there was just a warm-up for our proper discussion, which we would have to have outside on this very cold winter evening. We ordered our meal, and talked about trivial things. Ernest told me that he was organizing a football team in our Institute, and was very excited about it. But he didn't know with whom they could play because there was no other team in any of the Institutes. Finally we finished our meal, wrapped up in our warm winter coats and went out into the chilly winter night. We walked towards the Charles Bridge on Nerudová Ulice and Ernest asked me what I wanted to talk about. I started: 'England seems to me to be a wonderful country, and you know it too, Ernest, for you lived there. To have the freedom to work on any problem you want, and the fantastic benefit of the help of colleagues who are such brilliant scientists tempts me to live there.' 'Yes,' said Ernest, 'I can understand you and the fact that you were so impressed with the country, but here too we have a lot to be grateful for. We have a group of young colleagues, who are enthusiastic and committed to the work we do, and we are building something from scratch, so this is some compensation.' I agreed with that, but I had to tell Ernest that the main reason for my desire to live in England is my love (or infatuation) for Sidney and our wish to marry. 'Are you sure that you could leave your friends here and be happy living with Sidney in England? You know it can be very lonely, and it will be a difficult change for the children who are happy here.' said Ernest, 'Gerta you should think very hard about leaving home. Look, I lived in England for six years, and when I returned home I had a really difficult time finding a job and settling. Yet, I could not live anywhere else except here, this is my home, my country and my place is here. There could be no incentive for me that would entice me to leave Czechoslovakia. I can show you the poem I wrote when I returned home from England.' I never knew that Ernest was such a patriot, and this confession took me by surprise. It made me think about my own feelings and I tried to explain them to Ernest: 'It is different for me. I too was a patriot once, before the Holocaust; I felt that I belonged to Slovakia and that it was my home. But then my compatriots showed me quite clearly that they did not want me, and were prepared to send me off to die in a concentration camp, just to satisfy their greed. I can not feel loyalty to this country after the rejection I suffered. My roots have been brutally severed, and I can never be completely comfortable here. But Ernest I will take your advice seriously and give a lot of thought as to what would be best for my own and my children's future.' We reached the bottom of the hill, and were heading towards the Charles Bridge. We found the right stop for the streetcar that took me to my home, and Ernest boarded a bus. We separated and I felt happy that I had clarified some of the problems that I had, but my mind was not made up, and I knew that it would be a long time before I would be able to reach a decision. Also, I could not take the children away from Rudi their father, Tetinka and Ilonka, their grandmother.

There were so many things to consider, and our lives depended on my final decision, so I wanted the opinions of other friends. I thought that female friends might view my situation differently, and decided to talk to my friend Hanka, with whom I shared so many problems. She too was a single mother, her husband divorced her shortly before their son Jakub was born, and she had to fend for herself. Jakub was the same age as my oldest daughter Helena. We often took our children to various places such as the children's puppet theatre *Hurvínek and Špejbl* and other childrens' attractions. We also shared my baby sitter, Tetinka, and when Hanka and I went to the theatre Jakub came to our flat and slept over, while our Tetinka was baby sitting for all the three children. So Hanka understood very well how difficult it was to be a single parent, and how much I longed to have a partner I could share my life with. She also knew how I felt about my new relationship with Sidney, and the hopes I had that living with him would be the answer to my problems. I arranged to go out with Hanka on a Saturday afternoon and talk to her. She arrived to our flat with Jakub and the children were very pleased to be together while Tetinka supervised their games. We had a new toy, a medical kit, with a little stethoscope and toy syringes, and playing doctors was one of my daughters' favourite game, though Jakub complained that usually he had to be the patient.

Hanka and I went out to a nearby park, Stromovka, for my problems could be discussed only in the open, where I could not be overheard. Even at this time of the year the park was beautiful, a dusting of snow covered the trees, and this was particularly lovely on the few fir trees that were interspersed among the barren deciduous trees. The ground was frozen, and firm, not too slippery to walk on. We were dressed in warm winter coats, hats, gloves and felt boots so that although it was cold, we enjoyed walking in the park. I told Hanka that during my last trip to England Sidney and I decided we would like to live together and that I was thinking of leaving Czechoslovakia and moving to England. 'And how do you think you will accomplish this? They will never let you out with the children,' said Hanka. 'I know, but maybe we could go for a holiday to Yugoslavia and Sidney could arrange for a sailing boat to take us to Greece or Italy; from there we could go to England, or we could go to the coast in East Germany and somehow escape from there. Look Hanka, I don't have a clear plan, but I want to find out what I really want to do.' This was quite an accurate description of the state of my mind. Hanka looked at me and gave me one of her all knowing smiles, 'Gerta, deep down you already know what you want. You are passionately in love with Sidney, and of course you want to be with him. Don't pretend to yourself that you don't know what you want. However to achieve what you want is near to impossible. I know that you are being watched by the secret police, all your love letters are being censored, and the authorities must know that you want to get out.' I knew that Hanka was right, but still I said, 'I may as well try to go to Yugoslavia with the children for our next summer holiday. At present I haven't got the money to pay for it, but I do have my mother's expensive fur coat and I could sell it. I will start trying to find someone who would buy it straight away, and once I have the money I will book the holiday.' Hanka smiled and replied, 'It is a good idea to try, but I am sure you will not be allowed to leave even if you book your holiday and pay for it.' We left it at that and returned home to my flat in Dejvice, where we cooked something for supper and played with the children before Hanka and Jakub went back home. I did manage to sell the fur coat quite quickly, and the money I got was just about enough to pay for our holiday in Yugoslavia next July. I booked a holiday to Dubrovnik and the travel agency applied for a passport and exit visa on our behalf, to enable us to go. We were excited about going to the Adriatic Sea, the children had never seen the sea and I had only seen the Baltic Sea and the English Channel, which are quite different from the Adriatic. I had no idea whether we would be able to leave from Yugoslavia to Italy or Greece, but in any case I wrote to Sidney that we have booked our holiday to Dubrovnik and could he come and meet us there. I felt quite happy about this arrangement, and hoped that even if we were not able to leave for good we would have a good holiday. All I had to do now was to wait for the summer.

Trip to the Tatra Mountains.

But Sidney could not wait till our next meeting, in the summer and decided to take a study leave and work in Warsaw, Poland in the Nencki Institute. He went to Poland in February 1958, and we arranged to meet in April in the Tatra Mountains. Sidney's colleagues found us a room in the Polish resort of Zakopané. To travel from the Slovak part of the Tatra mountains to the Polish part it was not necessary to have a passport and all I needed was to appear at the border with my identity card and get a border pass that allowed me to stay on the Polish side of the Tatra Mountains for a few days. At the end of April I took a few days leave and we met at Zakopané. We stayed in a small house just outside Zakopané where a very nice peasant woman, Pani Pendzimanz, took care of us. The room we were renting was clean but very cold, and we had to curl up under a huge eiderdown to keep warm. During the day we took long walks. The mountain tops were still covered with snow, but in the valleys spring has taken a firm hold of the scenery with a dazzling display of colours and smells. The longest walk we took was to a lake called *Morskie Oko* which means 'the eye of the sea', a mysterious stretch of dark blue water, clear as a mirror so that the reflection of the surrounding mountains could be seen when the light was right. Maybe it all seemed so magical because we were together and in love, without a future to plan for, so the present time was all we had and the intensity of all our shared experiences was hugely amplified by this situation. The exhilarating walks in the mountains and the nights spent together loving each other passed too quickly and we had to separate yet again, hoping that we will meet in Yugoslavia in the summer.

Home again.

Back home after this short and intense holiday I felt an almost physical pain at being separated from Sidney. One evening when I was walking home from work with Ernest, I told him about my feelings. Ernest took my hand, and said: 'Gerta, please do not make any decisions yet, you are in an emotional turmoil, and blinded by passion. Please try to take control of yourself.' I knew he was right, but I could not do much about my feelings, and Sidney's daily letters telling me that he too felt it unbearable to be separated from me, kept my passion for him alive. Fortunately, my children were still the most important people in my life, and taking care of them was my priority and kept me sane. Preparations for the 1st of May celebrations were being made by all the Party members. On the 1st of May all the members of our Institute gathered in Wenceslas Square and marched through Prague, waving flags in front of our President, Antonín Novotný and other members of the government shouting appropriate slogans such as 'long live the President' 'long live the Soviet Union' and singing songs to show our loyalty to Socialist Czechoslovakia. This happened every year, but somehow this year it seemed to me quite ridiculous and inappropriate. After all we were adults and this seemed quite childish, and above all hypocritical. Hardly anyone wanted to wish a long life to Novotný, or any representative of our socialist government that had brought so much hardship to all of us. But no one refused to go to the demonstration, for that might have disastrous consequences, such as the loss of one's job and being sent out of Prague to some remote place without any possibility of work and income. So we put up with it, and didn't even openly question this stupidity. But for me it was just another illustration of the political situation in my country and another reason for wanting to leave.

July and the date for our holiday to Yugoslavia was getting close. I was excited about going to the Adriatic Sea with my children, and the possible escape. I made careful preparations, packed our best summer clothes and got the childrens' favourite toys ready. I still didn't have any travel documents though, and was impatiently waiting for them. And then three days before we were due to depart I got a letter from the travel agency saying that they were unable to obtain a travel permit for me and the children and that we were therefore unable to travel. I was shattered by the news, which showed that the authorities considered me as a suspicious person and would never give me permission to leave with the children. I had no answer to Helena's question: 'Mummy, why aren't we going to the seaside?' I think it was at this point that I decided to leave at all costs and not endure the constraints imposed upon me by the Communist Regime.

Chapter 13
Leaving Prague

An opportunity for escape.

The invitation to participate at a meeting in Poland to be held in the middle of September 1958, arrived in the spring. The programme for the meeting was interesting and I was delighted that the Czechoslovak Academy of Sciences agreed for me to attend it. The secretary of the Academy told me that my travel documents for the trip were ready. It was the beginning of September. I went to the Institute of Physiology where I worked, to find out whether my passport and train tickets for my trip to Poland had arrived from the Academy head office. It was warm and sunny, and as I walked from home to the Institute I was pleased that I could still wear my blue summer dress that I had made myself and was quite proud of. I entered the building where our Department was and headed for the administrative section. I liked the young, pretty secretary in the office and whom I knew quite well. When she saw me she smiled: 'I like your dress, it really suits you. I have good news for you, your passport and the return train ticket from Prague to Warsaw have arrived, Dr.Vrbová. I hope you will enjoy your trip.' And she handed me a brown envelope that contained these items.

Four of us from our Institute of Physiology were invited to attend the meeting in Poland on the topic of 'control of movement'. Colleagues from Russia and Hungary would also participate, and the scientific content of the meeting seemed to be very interesting. I was therefore pleased that I now had everything I needed to take part in this event. To be sure my documents were in order I checked my passport. While examining it I discovered that apart from the usual details about my date of birth, colour of eyes et cetera, my passport had on the third page a stamped exit visa, the wording of which caught my eye. It stated that I could go to Poland and return back through any country in Europe. This wording was unusual, since Czechoslovakia and Poland shared a border and there was no need to travel through any other country, but it meant that I could have a stop-over wherever I wanted and then perhaps not return at all.

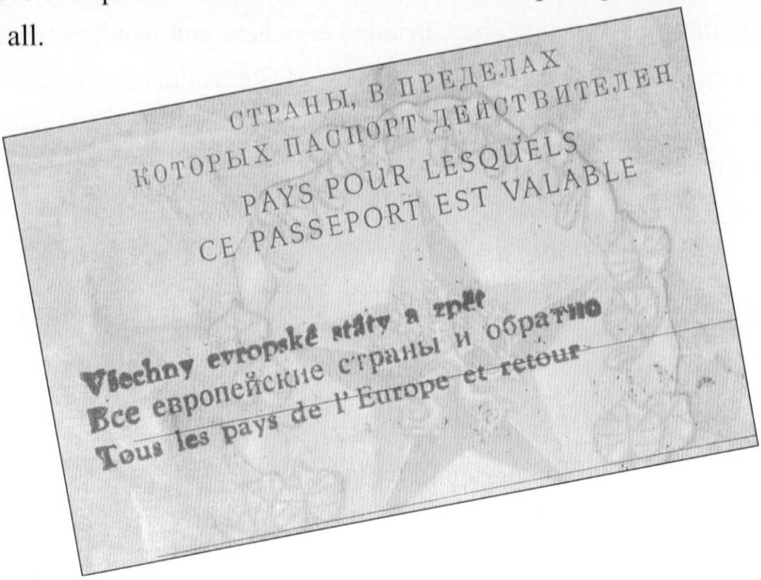

Page from my passport showing the crucial line: *Tous les pays de l'Europe et retour.*

But, the passport was still only in my name, and did not include the names of my two daughters. Thus in spite of this promising wording of the exit visa the problem of how to get my children out of Czechoslovakia was still unsolved. Nevertheless, some very exciting ideas about possible ways of leaving my country and moving to England with my children were constantly occupying my mind, and were in fact preventing me from thinking my scientific thoughts about work. I kept very quiet about it all and didn't talk to anyone about my schemes.

Before departing to Poland to attend the meeting I took my daughters to their childminder, Tetinka. We packed their things, and Helena insisted that her Elephant with a torn ear had to stay with her. Zuza took her enormous teddy bear and a small piece of silky material that she carried everywhere and handled before going to sleep. This rather filthy piece of silk had to be with her all the time. The week before I found out that I was going to Poland I went shopping to a store called *Dětský Domov* (children's home), where it was sometimes possible to buy children's clothes. I heard from my friends that the store had just obtained a consignment of children's underwear and I managed to buy new pyjamas for both girls. The girls insisted that they had to take these to Tetinka, and wear them while staying there. 'I will only be away one week, so it will not be long before I see you and we will be back home.' We walked across the road to Tetinka's flat. I found it hard to leave the children. I kept hugging them, and talking to them. Helenka had just learnt a new song about a swallow who realised that it is the end of the summer and will have to migrate south, but was sad to fly into the unknown. It started in Czech: *Uletěla vlaštovička, už je konec léta*, (the swallow flew away, it is the end of summer). I asked her to sing it for us, and I thought it was really appropriate for the occasion. Finally I managed to tear myself away from them and left to go home and pack my suitcase. Though I didn't know why, I had a premonition that this would be the last time I would leave my daughters in this little flat with Tetinka in charge.

With my suitcase packed, I took the tram to the main railway station and joined the other members of our delegation: Ernest Gutmann, Pavel Hník and Radan Beránek. Together we boarded the train to Warsaw. I wore a grey raincoat over my favourite summer dress and Beránek teased me that it could be cold in Poland, which is so much further north than Prague. My colleagues were full of enthusiasm and anticipation about the meeting where many new ideas were to be discussed, but I couldn't concentrate on anything else apart from hatching a scheme that would enable me to use this opportunity to escape from Czechoslovakia with my children. Yet I had to pretend to have no other thoughts than those about the meeting and the science to be discussed there.

We arrived at Warsaw late at night and we were met by our Polish colleagues, most of whom we knew from previous meetings. We were taken to the Nencki Institute and shown to guest rooms where we were to spend the night. The plan was, that the next morning we would visit the Institute and discuss the work that was carried out there. Later when other colleagues from Russia and Hungary had arrived we would board a coach and travel to a place called Osieczna, about 200 kilometres south west of Warsaw, where the Polish Academy of Science had a special venue for conferences.

Thus I had a day in Warsaw and a tentative plan for our escape started to take shape in my mind. The plan was as follows: provided

Sidney, could send me an air ticket for myself, Helena and Zuza to return from Warsaw to Prague via Copenhagen, I might be able to smuggle the children across the border to Poland, put their names on my passport and board a plane to Copenhagen. I wasn't quite sure how I would accomplish this, but it seemed a beginning of a plan. I chose Copenhagen rather than London, for I thought it would be less suspicious. So early the following morning after my arrival I went to the nearest post office and sent a telegram to Sidney in London to ask him to arrange a flight for Helena, Zuza and myself to travel from Warsaw to Prague via Copenhagen. I gave Sidney a *post-restante* address in a Warsaw post office from where I would pick up his reply. I made it clear that I needed the answer by the next morning, before departing for Osieczna.

Next morning I hurried to the post office and there was a telegram for me from Sidney, in English, stating that he had arranged for an airline ticket for me, Helena and Zuza to travel from Warsaw to Prague via Copenhagen to be collected from the Scandinavian Airlines (SAS) office in Warsaw. I was beside myself with joy but also apprehension, for the task of achieving our escape seemed just too great and too dangerous. Still the first step of our planned escape had been taken.

Later that morning all the participants of the meeting boarded a coach and we travelled to Osieczna. Throughout the journey I could think of nothing else but my escape. While doing so, I realized that in addition to a lot of luck I would need some help in Poland to carry out my plan. This meant that I had to confide in someone; and that was dangerous not only for me, but also for the person in whom I would confide. I knew several of my Polish colleagues from the

Nencki Institute, and I had to make up my mind who I should talk to and trust. I decided to discuss my plan with Andrzej, for I had met him at a previous meeting of our two Institutes that was held in the Tatra Mountains. We liked each other immediately and during a long walk together we discussed our personal problems and developed a very special empathy for each other. Andrzej also knew Sidney and was aware of our romantic involvement. Indeed, the previous May he had made arrangements for us to meet at the Slovak-Polish border in a Polish resort called Zakopané where Sidney and I spent a wonderful holiday in the house of an old peasant woman who took care of us. I was convinced that I could trust him, but I didn't anticipate the extent of the help he would finally give me.

Andrzej Zbrożyna (recent picture).

The house of the Academy in Osieczna was delightful. It was set in a deep forest next to a large lake. We arrived late afternoon and were given keys to our rooms at the reception. I shared a room with a young Polish colleague Eliszka. The air was still warm and balmy and Eliszka suggested that we should go for a swim in the lake immediately before dinner, even before we had taken our suitcases to our rooms. A few of us took our swimming costumes and towels and hurried to the lake. We waded in through the muddy bank and the water was soft as silk and warm. I swam with Eliszka, and for me the swim was important. It cleared my head and I could concentrate better on what to do next. On my way out of the water I brushed my leg against a tree branch and cut the skin on my left calf. The wound was not deep, but it bled a lot. Someone offered me a plaster and I used it to cover the cut. I was worried that my injury would interfere with my plans. But then I thought that my injury might come in handy and provide me with an excuse if I had to be absent from the meeting.

My Czech colleagues also came swimming with us and we walked back to the house together. I felt guilty for harbouring a secret, but at this stage I didn't want to involve them. Indeed I felt very lonely keeping my plan to myself. Back in the house we were shown our rooms. I changed for dinner and wore a smart little black dress with a very lovely amber necklace. We had dinner and it was an idyllic evening talking to friends and colleagues, yet I felt as taut as an overstretched string about to snap.

The meeting started next morning. The lecture theatre was pleasant, there were about 30 of us present. I was sitting next to a young Ukrainian scientist called Kostyuk who later became Head of the prestigious Institute of Neurophysiology in Kiev, and went on to play a leading role in developing Ukrainian physiology. I pretended to listen attentively to the talks, but was unable to concentrate. Fortunately, my Ukrainian neighbour produced a box of chocolates, opened it and offered me some. Eating chocolates calmed me a bit, and to Kostyuk's great surprise I soon ate all the chocolates in the box. He must have thought me really greedy! I managed to sit through the morning session, but by lunch I felt that I had to talk to Andrzej and ask for his advice. This I could only do outside, for the rooms in the building were probably bugged, and it was also risky to be overheard. Lunch was served in a great hall, with several large tables and chairs. I made sure that I sat next to Andrzej. While having lunch, I asked him: 'Would you come for a short walk with me after lunch?' He looked puzzled and a little curious, and in his usual pleasant manner replied: 'But of course, with pleasure.' So just before lunch ended we sneaked out of the dining room and headed to the woods. I didn't know how to start, but Andrzej made it easy for me and asked: 'What is troubling you?' and I explained: 'Andrzej, as you well know Sidney and I have been in love for two years now, and we would like to live together. I tried to get out of Czechoslovakia with the children, first by booking a holiday for us in Yugoslavia, then I tried the Baltic resorts in East Germany, but I could not get permission to leave Czechoslovakia with the children. The authorities know about my relationship with Sidney, I could not get permission to marry him or to leave the country to be together with him. I was watched by the secret police, my letters were censored and I am frightened. Having a close friend and lover from England is dangerous. My position will become even worse, for I know that the children's father Rudi is also planning to leave. Last weekend Rudi came and returned all the toys the children kept in his flat, and told me that he is going away to work in the Soviet Union for a year. When I asked around I found out that this is not so, but he is going to attend a Biochemistry meeting in Vienna at the beginning of September. He must be planning to stay in the West. With him abroad in the West it will be impossible for me to get away from Czechoslovakia together with the children, and without them I cannot live. From my war-time experience I have learned that nothing is impossible and that crossing borders illegally is not hard at all. So I have made a plan, and I would like to know what you think about it: Sidney is sending me air tickets to travel from Warsaw via Copenhagen to Prague. We would take a plane from Warsaw to Copenhagen but of course we would stay in Copenhagen and not return to Prague. But I will have to bring the children from Prague to Warsaw. I could go back to Prague illegally without having my passport stamped and without the authorities knowing that I am back. Then I would pick up my children in Prague and bring them back here to Poland across the mountains in the Krkonoše. I could take them to the top of Sněžka by cable car and chairlift and then walk them down the mountain to Karpacz Gorny, near Jelenia Gora. That is downhill, all the way, and I think we could manage it. What do you think about this plan?'

Map to show the border between Poland and Czech Republic.

Chapter 13

From behind his thick glasses Andrzej's grey eyes stared at me with amazement. It was at this stage that I realized how unrealistic and hazardous my plan was. Andrzej asked: 'Gerta, and how will you get the children's names entered in your passport?' 'Perhaps I will just enter their names into my passport myself,' I replied, 'I lived on forged documents for years during the war, I am sure this cannot be too difficult. Also Poland has a much more liberal administration since Gomułka took over power, so perhaps the people that check passports at the border will not look too closely.' (In 1956 after a bloodless revolution by the Polish Workers' Party, Władislav Gomułka became First Secretary of the Polish Communist Party. He called his policies *revisionist,* and introduced a more liberal government. This involved changes in the civil service and other government institutions). Andrzej took my hand and turned me around to face him: 'You are really serious about this? But if you leave the meeting here, people would report it and it will not take long for the authorities to find a Czechoslovak national travelling alone around Poland. I think this plan is impossible.' I replied: 'Yesterday, coming out of the lake I scraped my leg, not deliberately, but the injury may be useful and I can use it as an excuse to leave the meeting and say that I need to have my infected wound seen to in a clinic, possibly in Warsaw. I think this will delay any report that I left the meeting for some other reason. I can write and keep in touch with the meeting organisers, even send them a report from a clinic I will attend.' Andrzej sighed, and said: 'I can see that you are determined, and will not change your mind. But wait till tomorrow and I may come up with some ideas of how to help you. I don't think you can pull it off without help.' After that we returned to the meeting.

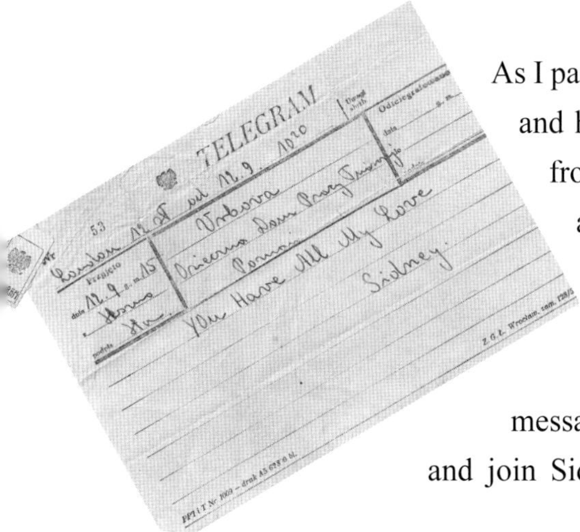

As I passed the reception, I was stopped and handed a telegram that was sent from England. I was apprehensive and quickly opened it. It was from Sidney and contained only one sentence: 'You have all my love. Sidney.' This simple message made my resolve to escape and join Sidney in England even stronger.

During dinner I was sitting at a table with my Czech colleagues. I felt that I had to tell my closest friend and mentor Ernest Gutmann of my intentions and find out what he thought. Not only because I knew that he would miss me and I too would find it difficult to be separated from him, but I also wanted to find out whether he was prepared to take the risks to his career and freedom that were connected with my escape. I knew that if my plans succeed the authorities would blame him for not being vigilant and allowing me to disappear to the West, and if I was to be caught he would suffer with me whatever charges and punishments I would have to face. Thus I had to see him on my own and tell him of my intention to escape.

After dinner I asked Ernest whether he would like to come for a walk with me and discuss the talk I was to give the next day. I think Ernest knew me well enough to feel that something other then my 'talk' was troubling me and probably guessed that I had some problems unrelated to my presentation at the conference. We went out into the warm evening and walked in the forest. It was Ernest who started the conversation: 'Gerta, what is worrying you? You seem so tense, what is the matter?' He looked so puzzled, his blue eyes behind his thick rimmed glasses showing fear and concern. 'Ernest,' I replied, 'I have decided to escape from Poland to England and I have a plan for bringing the children with me.' Then I told him what I intended to do. He didn't immediately question my plan, but was worried about my decision to go and live with Sidney. 'Are you sure you want to live with Sidney and bring the children to live with him too?' I was surprised at the question and replied: 'Ernest, you know I am madly in love with Sidney, and we have been going out together for two years, so why are you worried?' 'I am not sure that Sidney is the good person you believe he is and I don't think he will be a good father to your children. You are too blinded by your emotions, but I have been observing him, and I don't trust him. You are taking incredible risks escaping from Czechoslovakia, and even if you succeed with your plan, there is no way back for you, if things don't work out between you, Sidney and the children. It may appear to you that I am pointing these things out to keep you in Czechoslovakia and in the group, near to me; because we need you and you contribute a lot to the work. Also for me, you are such a dear close friend and I will miss our friendship. But this is not why I am warning you. I am really concerned for you and the children. You had a tough time, and Rudi was not an easy partner, or father. To risk living with another man, who may not be a good husband to you and a caring father to Helenka and Zuzka may not be a good idea. Also to take such horrendous risks for yourself and the children to be with him is too much.' I was so astonished by this conversation that I just blurted out: 'Why didn't you tell me this earlier?' Ernest was silent and then said: 'I didn't think that you would be able to leave in a hurry, and hoped that given time you would find out for yourself that Sidney does not deserve you. But now that you have made up your mind, Gerta I will support you and do whatever I can to help you to succeed with this crazy plan of yours. Just let me know what I can do.' 'Ernest, there is one thing I would like you to promise me.' I said this with great trepidation. 'In case I do not succeed, and get caught while trying to escape and would then be put to prison, or even worse, executed, will you please help to look after my daughters and make sure that they do not suffer too much.' I could hardly bear to think about this possibility, yet I wanted to make sure that my friends and people I trusted would be in charge of my children. Their father would probably not be in Czechoslovakia, so I had to involve friends. When I returned to Prague I would also ask the same thing of my friend Hanka. Ernest and I didn't want to stay out too long so we returned back to the building and mixed with other colleagues.

Returning to Prague to bring my daughters.

Back in my room I packed my bag and gave it to Andrzej to ask someone to take it to Warsaw. Next morning very early, Andrzej and I left the house in Osieczna. I left a note explaining that I had to see a doctor, because my leg was infected and very painful, and that I would return as soon as it had been seen to. Andrzej checked the train time table and we went to the railway station and took the earliest possible train to Jelenia Gora in the Krkonoše Mountains. From there we planned to climb to the top of a mountain, Sněžka, (meaning Snowcap), where it was possible to cross to the Czech side. I would take the chairlift and then a cable car down to a mountain resort called Pec and from there a coach to Prague to pick up my daughters. Andrzej was to come with me to the top, and from then on I would be on my own—crossing the border and going home to Prague. Andrzej would return to the Polish side and stay in a camp site in Karpacz Gorny.

We arrived to Jelenia Gora before lunch, took a coach to Karpacz Gorny and had enough time to reach the top of Sněžka by light, but we had to hurry. We bought some ham rolls and a bottle of water at a small café in Karpacz Gorny, and took this with us on our walk up the mountain. To reach the top in daylight we had to walk quite fast. It was a lovely sunny day, and the climb took hours. By the time we reached the top I was very tired. We had a look around the mountain top, entered the lookout tower where both Czech and Polish tourists could enjoy the view. After a brief inspection, we found a place where Andrzej could wait for my return with the children, without being too conspicuous. I was careful to memorize the spot, for I didn't want to have to search for Andrzej on my return with the children. I arranged to meet Andrzej either the next day, but more likely the day after, for I needed time to prepare for the journey. It was a lovely afternoon, there were many tourists walking on the top of the mountain around the lookout tower, and there was no problem crossing over to the Czech side of the mountain and getting on the chairlift down to Pec.

I arrived to Pec and got the next coach to Prague. It was getting dark when I arrived in Prague, and I knew it would be too late to pick up the children from Tetinka and bring them home. Also next day I wanted to be free to meet my friend Hanka and say goodbye. From the coach station in Prague I went straight back to my flat in Dejvice to make some preparations for my final departure from Prague. I let myself into the empty flat. Without the children it felt very lonely. It felt strange being back, and knowing that this is the last time I would see my home that I had put together with so much effort. Our flat was very small, the entrance hall that I converted into a kitchenette with a small cooker left just enough space for a slim person to turn around. The entrance to the bathroom was to the left and to the right the door lead to the children's room, (which was originally the kitchen). Everything in the flat was arranged to save space, and I liked the two beds for the children which could be folded away into a cupboard while the underside of the beds could then be used as a blackboard. There was a small table with two chairs in the middle of the room, where we could play and paint.

In my bedroom I sat down at my desk and switched on the lamp I had bought just a few weeks ago. I wished I could take it with me, it was really beautiful. And then there was the Indian silk carpet that my Uncle Arnold had given me as a wedding present and the peacocks in it were coloured by different shades of the most brilliant turquoise. Well I had to say goodbye to these few objects I liked, and resign myself to never seeing them again. But then during the war, I was so used to leaving things behind never to see them again that this did not concern me too much. I was though, deeply worried about the terrible risks I was taking with the safety of my children.

I was exhausted by the trip, the crossing of the border and the nervous tension I felt all the time; yet I was convinced that I was doing the right thing for the children and myself. Looking back on it I am amazed at my recklessness and audacity. If there is anything

I am ashamed of in my life it is this decision to expose my children to such terrible danger. Somehow at the time it looked different.

I went to bed and fell into a deep sleep. I woke early next morning. The weather suddenly changed and it was a dull and cloudy day, not good to go walking in the mountains. I took out my documents and put my medical degree certificate, and other official papers related to my divorce that I thought I might need into a folder. I looked through my photograph album, removed a picture of my parents and some pictures of the children and put them into an envelope. Then I went to the post office and telephoned my friend Hanka at the Institute, asking her to meet me for lunch. I had some time left, and spent it walking the streets of Prague, saying goodbye to my city.

Hanka and I met in a little café near my flat. She came on time and I was glad to see her. To me on that day she looked even prettier than usual. She wore her simple, shabby raincoat with grace and elegance as she walked towards me. Her calm brown eyes looked at me with some surprise: 'How come you are back? The meeting has not finished yet and all the others are still in Poland.' I realized she guessed that I came to pick up the children. I explained my plan to her, and I was grateful to her for not telling me that it was impossible and far too dangerous to succeed. Then I told her that I would like her to have my new camera, to take photos with it of our friends and her family, and send them to me to wherever I would be. Finally I came to the main point of our meeting. I took out a piece of typed paper that I had prepared in the morning, which stated that if anything would happen to me I entrusted the care of my children to her and handed it to her. 'Would you do this for me,

Hanka?' I asked. 'Ernest will help financially but I would like the children to be with you if I am arrested, or worse.' She promised to do her best, in case anything went wrong, but to my surprise she said with great confidence: 'I know your plan will succeed, and we will not have to resort to this.' Then she added: 'If you succeed, I do want to meet you, and we can always find some corner of the world where we can secretly meet. Don't forget, our friendship is for life, we can't stop now.' Her optimism and trust in our relationship gave me much courage. 'Do you think that you will have a lot of trouble from the authorities when I disappear to the West?' To this she shrugged her shoulders and said: 'I will manage.' We sat together for a while remembering many of our shared experiences such as holidays, visits to the theatre and other good things we enjoyed. Finally we got up, embraced and left the café.

It was now early afternoon, and I wanted to be with my children very badly. I walked the short distance to Tetinka's flat and rang the bell. She opened the door and with a happy smile let me in. Both my girls were playing in the sitting room, and when they saw me dashed to hug me. I never stopped marvelling at Helena's beauty. Her dark blue eyes examined the world with a shy and rather vulnerable expression, and her whole being was so gentle and quiet. On the other hand my younger daughter Zuza was mischievous and confident. No one expected me to be back so soon, and it was wonderful to have such a warm welcome.Tetinka asked why I had come home early, and I lied and said that the meeting was not very interesting, and I missed the children too much, so I had decided to return home. Tetinka gave me a brief account of what they were doing, and showed me some of the drawings they were getting ready for me. Helena drew pictures of the playground, swings and slides, and Zuza some abstract mixtures with lovely colours. Helena was to start school next week, and was very excited about it, and Zuza was to continue to spend her time with Tetinka. I told Tetinka that I wanted to spend a few days in the mountains with the children, a last vacation before Helena was to start school. 'I hope the weather will improve,' commented Tetinka. With that she turned and packed the few things the children had taken with them when they went to stay with Tetinka. I helped the children to put on their raincoats and outdoor shoes, the children gave Tetinka a big hug and kiss, and said they will see her in three days. I had to hide my embarrassment and keep a straight face for I knew that we might never see Tetinka again. I felt terribly guilty, for Tetinka loved my children and it would cause her much pain to lose them. But there was nothing I could do for it was too risky to tell the truth about what I was planning. Even much later I wasn't sure whether I would ever be able to explain to her why I inflicted this pain on her.

This was indeed the last time we saw her, but we haven't forgotten her for she played such an important role in our lives. And so we left Tetinka's flat and went home for the last time.

On arrival I cooked a meal for us. I had some schnitzels prepared and mashed potatoes and for dessert I mixed some cream cheese with sugar and an egg, for this was one of the few things that Zuza liked to eat. I explained to my daughters that tomorrow we must get up early, because we were going to go for a long walk in the mountains. I took the backpack out of the cupboard, and packed some essential things for the children; a change of clothes, warm tights, shoes, two light coats. I put the documents and photographs I had selected earlier into the backpack, and then there was no room for anything else. For the last time I made up the beds, the children changed into their new pyjamas, Helena hugged her Elephant with the torn ear and got ready to go to bed, and Zuza had her little piece of silk material that she had to handle before going to sleep. I read a bedtime story to the children before they went to sleep.

In my room, I rummaged through my papers and re-read some of the many love letters Sidney had written to me over the past two years. Since we first met he had written to me every day so there was a pile of letters in front of me, and I wanted to choose some of them to take with me. But then I changed my mind, for I felt the letters belonged to the rest of my things that I was leaving behind. I thought of our future life when we would finally be together, as I then believed forever. My children would have a better family life, and I believed a caring, loving step-father. I would make up to them for all the losses they suffered by leaving Tetinka and their friends behind, and hopefully we would find their own father, who would also be living in the West. Their future should be brighter in the West where there would be so many more opportunities for them. In short, I tried to convince myself that I was doing the right thing, taking them away in a most risky enterprise that could have disastrous consequences. I went to their bedroom, the night light dimly illuminated Helena with her thumb in her mouth and the Elephant in her arms, and Zuza clutching the piece of silk material in her hand and breathing calmly. I sat down on one of the two low chairs held my head in my hands and cried. What will become of us? What does the future hold for us? I wished I could have shared my worries about what the future had in store for us with Helena and Zuza. I asked myself if it was a good thing for them to tear them away from the life they knew, and take them into the unknown. I wished I knew what our lives would be like in 20 years from now. Would we be happy? I wondered. Finally there was no point tormenting myself with these questions, I went into my room, tidied up all the papers for the secret police to find, set my alarm clock so we could catch the earliest possible coach to Pec and went to bed.

Crossing the mountains to Poland.

Early next morning I woke my daughters and we dressed in warm clothes. Helena put on her green cardigan and Zuza her striped red and blue cardigan, both made of good quality British wool, presents from Sidney when he last visited us. We had a quick breakfast and set off for the coach station. When we were on our way, Helena suddenly stopped and said: 'We have to go back, I have left my Elephant behind!' I explained to her that we had no time to turn back and promised to get her an elephant later. We reached the coach station in good time and got seats on the coach. The children now started to enjoy the trip, and asked where we would be walking, and whether we would be meeting some friends.

We arrived at Pec just before lunch. There was a small restaurant near the coach station where we had some lunch. I was so nervous, I couldn't eat anything, but Helena who always liked her food had a good meal, some meat, red cabbage and really nice dumplings. Zuza, as usual, just picked at the food put in front of her, and said she wasn't hungry. I think she was apprehensive, and felt that something unusual was happening, but she didn't say anything.

It was a long walk from the coach station to the bottom of the cable car and by the time we reached the base station it had started to rain. The cable car went only half way up the mountain, and to reach the top we had to take a chairlift from a station half way up the mountain called Růžová Hora. The chairlift operated only in good weather and when it rained it was often closed for the final

Mount Sněžka

680 metre ascent to the top of Sněžka Mountain. The rain therefore was bad news, and I hoped that we would reach the chairlift base station, half way up the mountain, before the weather got really bad. When we reached the cable car, we were told that the chairlift was still operating, but might be closed down soon. There were few tourists taking the cable car, and with two small children I was quite conspicuous. But we got a lot of praise from our few fellow tourists for being really tough. Fortunately we had quite good rain-proof clothes and shoes. When we reached the top of the cable car at Růžová Hora we had to change onto a rickety, small chairlift. Fortunately, in spite of the bad weather it was still operating, but Zuza didn't want to sit down on it. There were two seats next to each other and when Helena saw that Zuza refused to sit down next to her she helpfully offered: 'I will go on my own, and you Zuza can sit on the other chair next to Mummy.' So Helena sat in front of me and Zuza next to me on the chairlift so I could put my arm around Zuza's shoulders to try and stop her from being frightened. There was a strong wind blowing the rain into our faces, and in spite of my efforts to calm Zuza

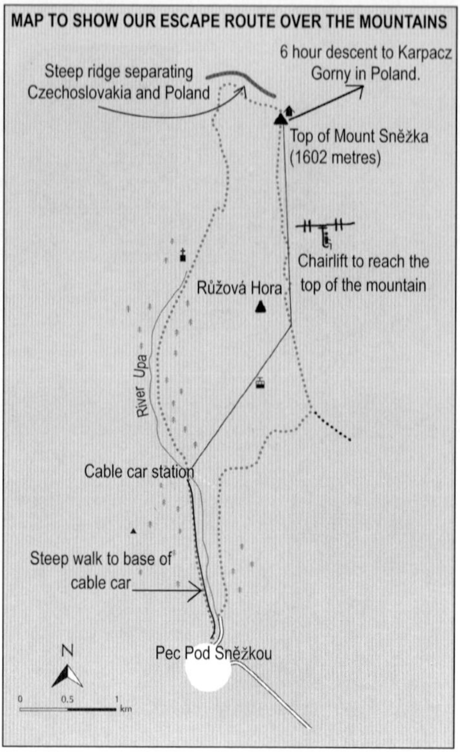

down, she was crying and shouting that she was frightened. Finally, we arrived at the top and were helped down from the chairs by a very friendly attendant.

The top of the mountain looked completely different from what it had looked like two days before, when it was bathed in wonderful sunshine. Now it was very misty and foggy, and the visibility was poor. Still, I hoped I would be able to find Andrzej at the place we arranged to meet. We entered the lookout tower and exited on the Polish side. I was worried that the children in their brightly coloured anoraks might be spotted by the guards but nobody noticed us, no one was looking in the pouring rain. 'We can't see any view,' complained Zuza, 'it is so misty and wet.' She was right, but to my great relief I did spot Andrzej waiting for us at the agreed place. I quickly introduced him to the children, and we set off straight away downhill.

The path was muddy and slippery, and we held the children by the hand. The rain made the walking unpleasant, and the slippery downhill path difficult to negotiate. Helena, quite sensibly, kept asking: 'Mummy, why aren't we going home? This is not a nice trip.' I thought that at this stage I couldn't answer that question, and felt ashamed. Zuza seemed to enjoy the descent, climbing down the steep, slippery rocks keenly. After the frightening experience with the chairlift, I could understand her; there was a romantic beauty in the misty mountain, with the remnants of the still vivid green colours of the leaves and trees. How symbolic, the heavy rain heralded the end of the summer and the end of our life in Czechoslovakia! However, in contrast to the countryside where it is certain that summer will be followed by autumn, we didn't know what to expect next. Andrzej was determined to get us down the mountain as fast as possible, and he walked at a brisk pace. Helena was getting very tired, and complained that she could not walk any more, while Zuza carried on. Finally, Andrzej took pity on Helena, lifted her on his shoulders and carried her. After a while I took over and we shared carrying her. Soon the enjoyment of being in the mountains faded away and we just carried on walking as fast as we could. We had to reach Karpacz Gorny from where the coach departed and would bring us to the railway station in Jelenia Gora, before it got dark and in time to catch the evening train from Jelenia Gora to Warsaw. So we marched on, in the pouring rain. Zuza was very brave, and walked unaided for the whole of the six hours it took

The Polish side of Mount Sněžka towards Karpacz Gorny.

us to reach the coach station in Karpacz Gorny. I hadn't realized the trip would be so strenuous, and without Andrzej's help I could have never accomplished it. Next to the coach station in Karpacz Gorny there was a small café, and we went in to get out of the rain. Before anything else, I took the wet clothes and shoes off my children and put on dry ones which I had taken with me in the backpack. Once the children were dry and warm they became interested in what was available in the café and noticed some very enticing cakes. Very politely, but in Czech they asked whether they could have some. Andrzej and I were frightened that someone might have heard them talking Czech, and we were delighted when the coach arrived before anyone noticed us. We boarded the coach and I promised the children that they will get cakes in Jelenia Gora.

Finally, we reached Jelenia Gora. We went to the station and Andrzej went to enquire about the train's departure time and bought tickets for us. We had about one hour to spare and went to the restaurant in a hotel opposite the station. We ordered hot soup and cakes. The refreshments helped, and we were feeling better. It was now getting dark and time to board the train.

Andrzej did all the talking, and asking questions about the journey, and the platform from which the train to Warsaw was to depart. The three of us just followed. We had to be quiet, for it would have been dangerous if someone had noticed that we were Czech. It was lucky that the children were very tired, too tired to ask questions or show too much interest in what was going on. Andrzej found us a compartment that was empty, and we could settle down there. On either side of the compartment there were wooden benches, long enough for Helena and Zuza to lie down, and leave enough room for Andrzej and me to sit down by the window. My anorak was dry by now and I covered Helena with it and Zuza was covered by Helena's and her own anorak. The compartment was cosy and warm, and we were relieved when the train started to move and left the station. We switched off the lights and tried to sleep. The most dangerous part of our crossing was over, and we thought that the further we were from the border the safer we would be. All of us were exhausted, the children soon fell asleep, but I was too nervous to sleep. I think this was also true of Andrzej, for he too was awake for a long time. Just as I was dozing off, the door of our compartment opened, and in the light that filtered into the compartment from the well lit corridor we could see a man entering our compartment. Andrzej was wide awake, and I realized that he was frightened. Like me he thought that somebody had spotted us, and had followed us and that we would be arrested. But the man just stood in the door, took in the scene with the sleeping children and us squeezed at the end of the seat, apologized, walked out and closed the door behind him. After this shock both Andrzej and I went to sleep.

Final stages of our escape.

I woke up just before the train pulled into Warsaw's central station, and started to worry about the next steps of my plan. Both, Helena and Zuza were still asleep, but Andrzej was awake. Talking in a very low voice I asked Andrzej, 'Where will we go when we arrive in Warsaw? We cannot go into a hotel—that would be too dangerous.' Andrzej had it all worked out: 'My sister-in-law is a sculptress, she has a large studio, where she works, and you and the children can stay there. I have asked for her permission, and she has agreed. I will bring some sleeping bags for the three of you and you can stay there until you leave.' Suddenly the list of errands I would have to make in Warsaw to arrange the next steps of our escape seemed enormous, and with the children with me I was worried that I would not be able to manage. But there was no going back, and I had to work things out as best as I could. I knew that I would need much help from Andrzej and my Polish colleagues. We arrived to Warsaw on a grey, misty morning, and the city seemed very alien to me. The children were pleased to finally get off the train, and excited to walk the streets of a new place that they didn't know. Andrzej got us tickets and we took a tram that took us to a block of houses, where Andrzej's sister-in-law, Barbara, had her studio. We were very disappointed and worried when we found that Barbara wasn't there. Fortunately, Andzrej had a reserve plan. His brother Jacek had a flat nearby and he agreed that we could come and stay there during the day. He also promised to look after the children and take them to a playground while Andrzej and I went on our errands to arrange our departure. Our first job was to pick up the air tickets from the Scandinavian Airlines head office and book the flight to Copenhagen. The next task was to forge my passport and enter the children's names in it.

For that we needed the right coloured ink and an ink eraser. Then I had to go to the Danish consulate and get a transit visa to travel from Warsaw to Prague through Copenhagen. I was anxious to complete all these arrangements on the same day, for the longer we hung around in Warsaw the more dangerous it would be for us.

As soon as Jacek, Andrzej's brother, took the children to the playground Andrzej and I went to the Scandinavian Airlines head office in the centre of Warsaw. The tickets were waiting for us, and I booked the only flight for Copenhagen next day, which departed from Warsaw in the late morning.

We found a stationer's store where we bought ink, pens and an eraser and went to Andrzej's office at the Nencki Institute. All the details in my passport were entered in Czech as well as Russian. We had to painstakingly copy each individual letter from the existing text in Czech and Russian from my passport and then write the names of Helena and Zuzana both in latin and cyrillic alphabets in the appropriate section of my passport. Then we had to use the eraser to remove a line and replace it by 'and two children' at the right place of the exit visa. It was a rather bad forgery, but neither Andrzej nor I were experts.

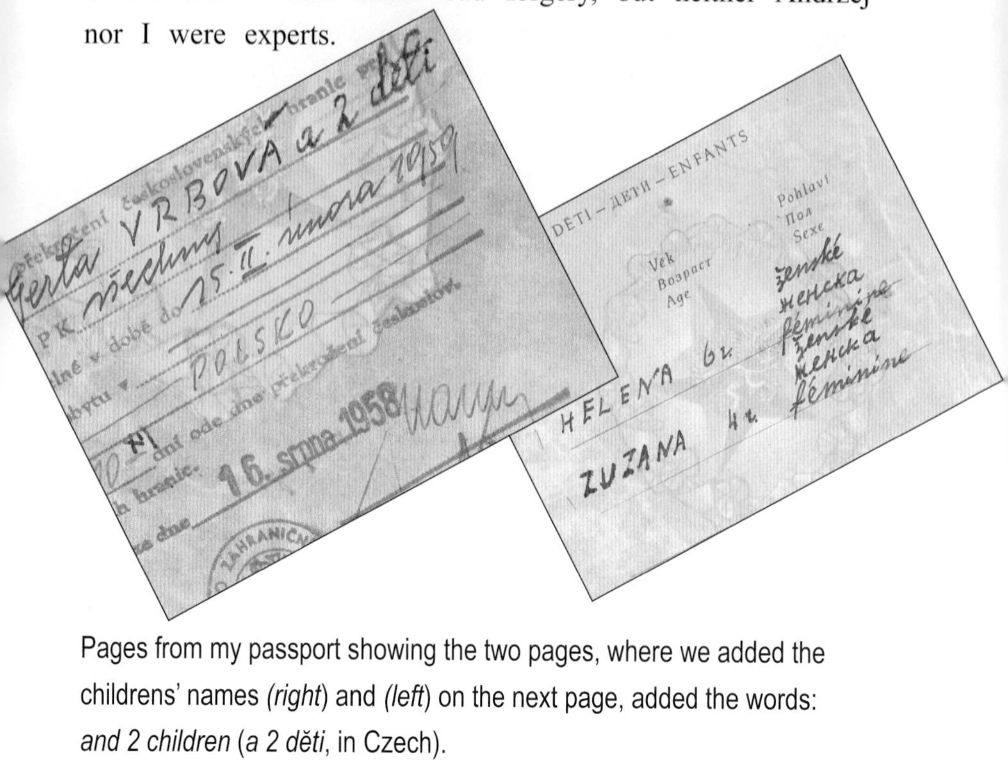

Pages from my passport showing the two pages, where we added the childrens' names (*right*) and (*left*) on the next page, added the words: *and 2 children* (*a 2 děti*, in Czech).

When the work on my passport was complete I set off to the Danish Consulate with my passport and the air tickets, and Andrzej went to Jacek's apartment to help with the children. Later, I learned that Jacek reported that they were squabbling and he had difficulties communicating with them, but at the time I didn't know about this and concentrated on the next step of the mission—getting the Danish visa.

This phase of our escape was the most dangerous, because now that my passport was forged, there was no way I could talk my way out of the situation. I arrived at the Danish Consulate just before closing time and I was the only applicant for a visa. A friendly young man took my passport, and thought that it was unusual to travel through Copenhagen to Prague and stay for only 24 hours. I explained that I always wanted to see Copenhagen particularly the Mermaid, and that 24 hours is better than nothing. He smiled pleasantly, and asked me to wait while he telephoned the Czechoslovak Embassy to make sure that my passport was valid for travelling through Denmark. At that moment I nearly fainted, and it took all my willpower to appear calm. I listened to the telephone conversation, but wasn't sure what the answer was, until the young Dane put the phone down, smiled at me and said that everything was OK. He then stamped the visa into my passport allowing me to stay in Denmark for 24 hours. I was shaking all over when I walked out of the Danish Consulate, but I had my passport with the children's names in it and a Danish visa.

I made my way back to the flat where we were staying and couldn't wait to see the children. They were there with Jacek waiting for me, and missing me. Andrzej was out getting our sleeping bags and some supper. I told Jacek and the children that we were leaving the next day and will be flying to Copenhagen. Hearing about the prospect of flying to Copenhagen was exciting news for the children.

Meanwhile Jacek's wife, Barbara, appeared and we moved into her *atelier* where we were to spend the night. Andrzej went to get us some sleeping bags and sandwiches, and when he returned with these items he also had some news. 'The meeting in Osieczna finished today,' he said. 'Everyone accepted that your leg needed to be treated and no one reported you missing.' This was a great relief. Then he continued: 'Gerta, some members of the Konorski's team would like to come and see you off at the airport. They think that it will be less dangerous for you if you are seen off as an official guest of the Academy by your colleagues. I think they are right.'
I was not so sure: 'What if someone reports me to the Secret Service?' I asked. Now that several people knew about my plan I was worried. Andrzej looked offended: 'No Polish colleague would do such a thing.' he replied. I felt embarrassed, and wished I could say the same about my Czech colleagues, about whose honesty and loyalty I was not so sure of.

Then we ate our supper, and I repacked our things and put all our possessions in the one suitcase I had brought with me from Prague. I didn't want to take the backpack with me to the airport, I thought it might be suspicious. I had had a long day and was exhausted. The children crawled into their respective sleeping bag, Andrzej went home and I too crawled into my sleeping bag and fell asleep, surrounded by Barbara's statues.

I woke up to become aware that a decisive day was about to begin when the success of all my efforts would be tested. I had exposed my family to so much danger and only now would I know whether my plan had worked. If so, I should be in Denmark by this afternoon and start a different life. But we still had to get through this morning. Helena was the first to open her large blue eyes and looked around the strange room. I went to her gave her a hug and was so pleased to feel the warmth of her body against my skin. I so much wished that I was guiding her to a better life, but only future years could tell that. Zuza was still asleep, so I used the time just to lie close to Helena and enjoy the intimate closeness between us, her soft arms around my neck. Finally, Zuza too opened her eyes, and I went to give her a cuddle. 'Time for breakfast,' Helena said, and climbed out of her sleeping bag. We washed and dressed and had something to eat. Then I completed the packing, folded the sleeping bags, and sat down with the children to play some games. We were ready to leave when Andrzej arrived to take us to the airport. The children were excited about travelling on an aeroplane but my legs felt like jelly at the prospect of using the forged passport to get across passport control. My only hope was that Poland's new administrators installed by Gomułka might not try hard to be efficient about some Czechoslovak mother leaving Poland with her children.

We arrived at the airport about one hour before the plane was due to depart. To my great surprise several of my colleagues from the Nencki Institute were already there waiting for us with flowers, and small presents for the children. I was moved to tears at the risk they took, but it calmed me down and helped me to face the official who checked my passport. He was friendly, smiled at the children and said: 'It is nice to see someone who travels with children, we hardly ever see any children travelling with their parents.' This was a really surprising comment, but pleased me no end. He hardly looked at my passport, but was looking at my colleagues, who were crowded around us, kept hugging me and the children and bidding us a very emotional farewell. Thus we passed the passport control without any difficulty and found ourselves in the departure lounge. After a short while our flight was called and the three of us went towards the Scandinavian Airlines plane which was already boarding. We reached the bottom of the steps and to my surprise a very morose person in uniform was checking passports of all the passengers. I handed him the passport, and he started to examine it. Without any encouragement the children ran past me, up the stairs into the plane and excitedly shouted: 'Mummy, this is so smart and wonderful, come and have a look!' The man tried to call the children back, and they descended a few steps towards me. I couldn't allow this to happen, and quickly snatched the passport from the man's hand and said: 'I have to look after the children,' and dashed up the stairs into the aircraft which was Scandinavian territory and where we were safe.

Repercussions of our escape.

It wasn't till much later that I found out what had happened to my friends and colleagues when the Czechoslovak authorities realized that I had escaped, taking the children with me. More recently I got the transcript of the proceedings against me conducted by the Czechoslovak government after my illegal escape. From this, and various other information, I found out that my Czech colleagues who were with me in Poland were severely reprimanded for having failed to report my disappearance from the meeting to the Polish authorities. For this they were punished by having their travel abroad curtailed. Ernest Gutmann was not allowed to travel anywhere for several years after I had escaped. My friends and particularly Ernest Gutmann were interrogated by the secret police and accused of disloyalty to the state and lack of vigilance for failing to report my intentions to leave the country. Fortunately there was no evidence that any of them had any knowledge of my intentions, indeed their testimonies agreed that as far as they knew Sidney and I wanted to settle in Prague. This seemed obvious to Gutmann, since Sidney had enquired about possibilities of obtaining a job in Czechoslovakia after his divorce. The authorities were also puzzled by the fact that my ex-husband Rudi Vrba did not return from a meeting held in Vienna and had emigrated to Israel at exactly the same time as I and the children escaped through Poland to Denmark. They could not believe that this was a coincidence, but strange as it may sound, it really had been a coincidence.

Fortunately, since there was no evidence that anyone knew about my intentions to escape, no serious proceedings could be launched against any of my friends and colleagues. The testimonies of my neighbours about my behaviour varied, the only reports that were damaging were those claiming that I often had foreign visitors staying in my flat. Most of the neighbours and particularly Tetinka were loyal to me.

According to the transcript of the proceedings against me, after my disappearance, the police needed access to my flat and the reason given for obtaining it was that my party card had to be retrieved, for if this got into the wrong hands it could be damaging to the country. Thus the Secret Service officials got the keys to my flat from Tetinka and in the presence of a reliable party member, Olga Hudlická, entered it. I had left the card on my desk, so this was retrieved, but a detailed inventory of all my possessions had to be carried out. Reading through the list of my possessions now, 50 years later, was an amusing experience; all the items listed were described as old, threadbare and thus worthless. Obviously a precaution against my ever claiming any compensation for confiscated goods. The only thing that Tetinka managed to rescue from under the watchful eyes of the officials, who ransacked my flat, was a single slipper of Helenka's. The Secret Service tried to figure out how I escaped, but got it wrong. They knew that I took the children to Poland illegally, but thought that I did so by crossing the Tatra Mountains in Slovakia and never discovered that I took a much more comfortable route via the chairlift in Krkonoše. It probably didn't matter. The final verdict against me was four years imprisonment and four years loss of civil rights. Fortunately this could not be enforced, for I was out of the clutches of the Czechoslovak authorities, and the verdict was revoked when the new democratic government took power in 1989.

I was sorry for the suffering and stress I caused my friends, but in spite of this we managed to maintain our friendship and affection for each other throughout the years. I am very grateful to them for this gift.

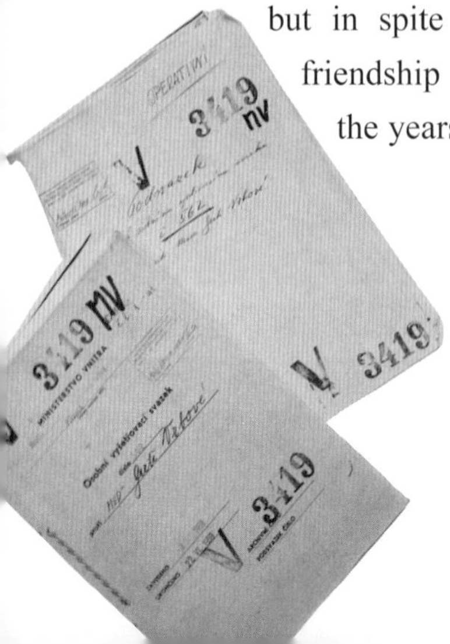

Left Secret Service dossiers: interviews with Tetinka and my friends and colleagues; list of contents of our apartment; conclusion that we had escaped via a place in Slovakia.

Chapter 14
Denmark

Arriving in Copenhagen.

Our plane from Warsaw landed at Kastrup Airport in Copenhagen in the early afternoon of September 20th 1959. My daughters Helena and Zuza were avidly examining the airport which looked luxurious compared to the airport in Warsaw from where we had set off just a few hours ago. After collecting our small green suitcase we went through passport control. To my amazement the immigration officer glanced just briefly at my passport and waved us through the barrier. We were now officially in Denmark. At the exit I spotted Sidney and another handsome man, who turned out to be Sidney's Danish friend Morten. I held my children by their hand. My palms still sweaty from the fear I had felt throughout our journey. The irrational feeling that somehow the Czechoslovak Secret Service would discover that we were on the plane, kidnap us and take us back to Czechoslovakia, where I would face prison and lose my children would not leave me. Although I felt that by entering Denmark the distance between the three of us and the 'Czechoslovak danger zone' increased, I still could not believe that we were safe. My pent up tension lessened as I fell into Sidney's arms. He drew me close and whispered: 'Don't worry, we are together now and can start a new life. You are safe, and I will do all I can to make us happy. Relax now and later you have to tell me all about your escape, how you managed to cross the border between Czechoslovakia and Poland and get here safely together with the children. I am proud of you that you managed it.' I looked into his pale and tired face, with rings of fatigue under his eyes, and knew that he probably had not slept much since he sent us the air tickets six days ago, and knew of the dangerous border crossing the three of us had taken. He released me from his embrace, turned to Morten and introduced us: 'This is Gerta, Helena and Zuza. I told you about their ingenious escape from Czechoslovakia, and now, at last they are here.' Then Sidney turned to me and added: 'Morten is an old friend, an immunologist, a very active member of the movement *Science for Peace* (an organisation that had been trying to develop good relationships between scientists all over the world and encourage them to collaborate). Morten smiled at us and said: 'Sidney and I hardly slept while waiting for you and what a relief it is to have all three of you in Denmark, where we can help to take care of you.'

Morten had his car at the airport car park, an old maroon vintage Bentley and all of us squeezed in. It was a clear sunny day as we drove past the centre of Copenhagen to Klampenborg, a beautiful district close to the sea. We saw large luxurious houses with well kept gardens close to sandy beaches. I had never seen such a well tended residential area anywhere. Morten explained: 'You are going to stay in Klampenborg, in the house of a friend of mine, Dr. Skinhöj. He has a small basement flat and you can stay there until you get your visas to England. I guess that is where you are heading.' 'Yes you are right, Morten, I hope Gerta and the children will be able to come with me next week.' My English was not good enough to follow the conversation, but I got the gist of it.

The area we were passing through was truly lovely. Apart from the luxurious elegant houses we could see the sea and sandy beaches. The light in this northern city was quite different from the one I was used to in *Mitteleuropa*. The sky was paler, and in spite of the sun everything was a little hazy.

Morten's Bentley stopped in front of one of the houses, and we entered. Morten had the keys to the house, unlocked it and lead the way down some stairs, to a small basement flat, with a tiny kitchen, a small sitting room a good sized bedroom, and a well equipped bathroom. In fact, this flat was larger then the one I left behind in Prague. We took our suitcase and Sidney's small holdall from the car and carried it to the flat. Morten brought a large brown paper bag. In the kitchen he handed it to Sidney and said: 'I brought some food for you, so tonight you don't have to go out for dinner or shopping, I guess you are tired and will want to talk and rest. It must have been a trying time for all of you and you probably want to be alone. I will go home now and will see you tomorrow.' He was gone before I could thank him, and now we were alone, me, the children and Sidney. We looked into the brown bag, and found that Morten bought us a most delicious selection of *smorebrod*—smoked eel, ham, eggs and herrings and for the children bread with chocolate spread and bananas. That indeed was a treat, for back home in Czechoslovakia luxuries like chocolate spread or bananas were unavailable. We ate our meal and then I took the children's pyjamas out of the suitcase, encouraged them to undress, have a quick wash put on the pyjamas and go to bed. The beds were made up for them, they had comfortable duvets and I was hoping they would fall asleep instantly. But this was not to be. Helena started to cry and demanded her Elephant with the torn ear and Zuza joined in and wanted her teddy bear. My hugs and promises to find them similar toys tomorrow had little effect, and I realized that all of us had a very difficult time ahead of us, missing our home and all the familiar things we loved. Finally after listening to several of my stories I made up specially for them, they fell asleep.

Now Sidney and I were alone and for the first time since we met we felt awkward and inhibited. We longed to make love but were emotionally exhausted, and when we undressed and went to bed we could only lie still, holding each other, and thinking of the enormity of the responsibilities we had undertaken by this irreversible move. We knew that our lives had now changed forever and I had some fears about the future, but this was overcome by the joy of being at last together with Sidney.

Next morning we got up, had breakfast and waited for Morten to turn up. While we waited I told Sidney some of the details of our border crossing. I also mentioned that without Andrzej's help we could not have accomplished it. Sidney recounted his worries during the past week: 'After I got your telegram from Warsaw, which was about a week ago, I couldn't sleep, I was so worried about you. I don't think I have had a night's sleep since I knew that you are taking such risks coming here. I came to Copenhagen to make sure that when you arrive here in Copenhagen with the children, all will be arranged for you here. Morten was fantastic and helped me with everything. It just shows how important friends are in life.' I couldn't agree more with this statement.

When Morten arrived, I had to go to the Danish immigration office to extend my visa which was valid for only 24 hours, and then I had to find an elephant for Helena and teddy bear for Zuza in Copenhagen's toy shops. It took only a few minutes to have my visa extended for a six week stay, but the search for the elephant and teddy bear was much more difficult. Morten and Sidney left the children and me in one of Copenhagen's main shopping areas. Sidney gave me some money for the toys and Helena, Zuza and I set out to explore the toy shops. We sampled the soft toy department in several of the shops, saw several elephants and teddy bears that seemed to me to be a suitable replacement of the toys we left at home. Zuza chose a small brown teddy bear with a pink bow round his neck and was pleased to cuddle it, but there was no elephant that would appeal to Helena. We went to countless shops, and sampled what seemed to me, all the toy elephants in Copenhagen, but none of them met with Helena's approval. None of them had a torn ear, or the colour of the fur that her old Elephant at home had. Helena was devastated and cried that she missed her Elephant too much, could not stay here in Copenhagen without it and had to return home to get it. I was painfully aware of her longing, not only for her Elephant but for the life we had left behind.

She must have been intuitively aware that there was no return in the foreseeable future, and was apprehensive of our new life. It wasn't just the Elephant with the torn ear she was missing, but everything and everybody we had left behind; Tetinka, Ilonka the children's grandmother (Babička) and all our friends, many of whom we might never see again. These were difficult hours when we were mourning all the love and friendships we had our little flat and embarked on our journey to Denmark and our new life in the West. The unsuccessful search for the Elephant and Helena's mood, made me feel guilty about the decision I had taken to leave Prague.

Our immediate practical problems overshadowed these concerns. We met Sidney and Morten in a coffee bar in the town centre, had something to eat and discussed what to do next. Sidney had to go back to London in two days' time, but we could not join him, for we had no British visa, so we would have to be separated yet again.

The next two days went by very quickly, I spent my time trying to familiarise myself with my new surroundings, and entertain my children. Sidney and I discussed the next steps we had to take to get visas to England so that we could finally be together. Sidney was confident that he would be able to obtain our British visa within a few days, so we expected our stay in Copenhagen would only be a few more days. I had my original valid air ticket from Warsaw to Copenhagen and back to Prague. The plan was that as soon as I had received my British visa, I would change the destination of the last leg of the journey from Copenhagen to London. Sidney had to leave Copenhagen, and Morten drove us to Kastrup Airport. We said goodbye to Sidney, expecting that this time it would only be for a few days. I felt very lonely. Morten was with us and I was grateful to him, for we needed his support. He dropped Helena Zuza and I off in our small place in Klampenborg, and I tried to plan my next few days alone with the children. Morten had pointed out an enticing playground nearby, close to the beach and I thought we could go there tomorrow; I was emotionally drained, but did not want the children to notice how tired and worried I really was.

Exploring Copenhagen.

The next few days seemed to drag on indefinitely. There was no news from Sidney about our English visas and Copenhagen's beauty and charm were wasted on me, though I tried bravely to appreciate them. The first day after Sidney left, instead of going to the playground, we spent most of our time again trying to find an elephant Helena would accept. We walked along rows of shops in expensive Östergade (now Ströget, part of a pedestrian district), reached the elegant Hotel d'Angleterre and found an enormous store, the *Magasin du Nord*. Surely, in this large and elegant store there must be an elephant Helena would like? In the soft toy department the shop assistant produced at least 30 elephants of various colours and sizes and Helena scrutinized each of them with an intense look of her dark blue eyes. Zuza enjoyed walking around the store, and admired several toys. I promised her that as soon as I had some more money I would buy her some. But Helena, rejected all the elephants, to the dismay of the shop assistant, and was not interested in sampling any other toys or items.

It seemed to me that so far all I had seen in Copenhagen were department stores, and I felt enough was enough, and that we deserved a tour of the harbour and a proper view of the Mermaid. I managed to persuade the children that a boat trip would be exciting, and interesting. The following day the weather was perfect for such a trip and we took the tram from Klampenborg to Nyhavn from where boats departed at regular intervals to cruise along the harbour, taking in Slotsholmen, Christianshaven and the Little Mermaid perched on a rock. Both the girls knew the story of the Mermaid and were excited to see her sitting there. All three of us enjoyed the cruise, for Helena and Zuza this was the first time they had been on a boat on the sea. The trip took my mind away from the problems I faced.

It was already one week since Sidney had returned to England, and the news was bad: the Home Office in England was unwilling to grant us immigration visas as refugees from Czechoslovakia. The only way we could get visas was if Sidney married me, but he was not free to do so, for his divorce had not yet been finalized. I had no idea what I would do, if I had to stay in Copenhagen alone with my two children without a job and support. And in the end that was exactly what happened.

Morten was our regular visitor and helped us as much as possible, but as the days passed and there was no news about our English visas, my nerves were beginning to be more and more frayed and my patience was running out. We had now been in Copenhagen for over one month living in limbo, not knowing how much longer we would have to wait before being allowed entry to England. The weather was changing and instead of bright sunny days most of the time the sky was heavy with dark clouds and it rained almost every day. We had no suitable clothes and were cold. We couldn't settle in Copenhagen for we had no idea how long we would be there. It was extremely hard for my daughters, for although with Morten's help I tried to pretend that our stay in Copenhagen was a sort of holiday they missed other children's company, and a feeling that they belonged somewhere. Finally, exactly one month after we had arrived to Copenhagen, it was time to take some action and resolve the situation one way or another.

Invading Britain.

I was rather naïve and thought that if I just turned up in England with my good professional qualifications two small children, a 'fiancé' who would promise to take care of us, and the romantic story of our love for each other across the Iron Curtain, we surely would be allowed into the country.

In a nearby travel agency I changed our air tickets and instead of the booked flight from Copenhagen to Prague I booked a British Airways flight from Copenhagen to London to depart in two days time. I telephoned Sidney to tell him of my decision and gave him the time of our arrival and flight number from Copenhagen to London. He knew that we would arrive to Heathrow Airport on a British Airways flight on the 21st of October 1958, almost one month after we had arrived in Copenhagen from Warsaw. I sensed that this news somewhat alarmed Sidney, and he didn't share my optimism about the British Home Office and Britain's immigration policy. But I was impatient and felt that our situation had to be resolved one way or another.

On the morning of the 21st of October Morten, yet again, drove his Bentley with the three of us to Kastrup Airport to get our flight to London. All went smoothly, nobody questioned us as we boarded our flight to London. The plane landed at Heathrow, in the early afternoon. We collected our luggage and went to the counter marked PASSPORT CONTROL. I produced my special Czech passport which of course did not include a British visa. The official at the counter was rather surprised, and told me that he could not let us through the passport control without a valid British visa. He took us to a small room and told me to wait for someone to come and talk to me. By that time the children were becoming impatient and worried, and it was difficult to calm them down. After waiting for some time, a well dressed and pleasant man came to talk to me. 'Dr. Hilton is waiting outside and has explained the situation to me,' he said, 'but we cannot admit you to Britain without a valid visa. Dr. Hilton persuaded us that due to the special circumstances and his intention to marry you as soon as he is free to do so, we are to contact the Home Office Secretary, who may grant you special permission to enter the United Kingdom. This will take some time, and you and the children will have to stay overnight at the airport in a flat especially reserved for illegal immigrants. You will be allowed visitors, and Dr. Hilton is already waiting outside to meet you.'

Within a few moments Sidney entered the room and I felt that now all our problems will be solved. He put his arms around me and just having him near made me feel safe. But then he explained that in spite of all his efforts, he was not sure that we would be allowed into England. 'I contacted my MP and he, in turn, got in touch with the Home Secretary, R.A. Butler. My promise to marry you after my divorce though, is not good enough, and the fact that we want to live together while I am still married is not in our favour. You see this is still a very puritanical society that does not approve of unconventional relationships. Still, maybe the Home Secretary will be sympathetic.' I was impressed and pleased that Sidney had gone to so much trouble and worked so hard to help us to get into England and be together, but his view of British attitudes disturbed me. While Sidney and I discussed our options, a young woman came and told us that she would now take us to the little apartment where the children and I would stay over night. All of us followed her, and she showed us into a pleasant small studio flat with a bedroom and kitchenette. She made us tea and produced some cakes, which was a very welcome interruption, for while I had no appetite, the children were hungry.

While we were having tea another visitor arrived; Sidney's mother Betty came to meet us. She was a very well dressed elegant lady in her early 60s and I was pleased that she had made the effort to come to see us. She brought a whole selection of toys and picture books for the children. Although Betty and the children could not understand each other they communicated well using simple body language, and Helena and Zuza were delighted to meet her. It was a good start for what turned out to be a long lasting relationship later, when all of us finally lived in England. Betty apologized that Sidney's father was unable to come, and told me that he would have loved to have met us. Thus it was in our little prison at Heathrow Airport that we first made contact with Sidney's family.

It was late afternoon when Sidney and his mother left us. We were given a light supper, and went to bed. The children quickly fell asleep but although I was very tired I couldn't sleep, for I was worried about our future.

Next morning we woke up and had breakfast. We had the most delicious croissants I had ever tasted and real coffee. The children had orange juice and cornflakes as well and even years later remembered the sumptuous breakfast provided courtesy of Heathrow Airport immigration authorities. But after breakfast things were not so good. Sidney arrived at around 9 o'clock in the morning and told us that we have to wait for the Home Secretary R.A. Butler's decision about our visa and that we will not know about the result untill after 10 o'clock am. The waiting seemed endless. We played with the children but the minutes dragged on and we were still uncertain what will happen to us. Finally the same immigration officer who had talked to us the day before, came into the room, and as soon as I saw him I knew the news was bad. He sat down and with slight embarrassment said: 'I am sorry, but your request for an entry visa was rejected by the Home Secretary. The reasons given by you and Dr. Hilton stating your intent to marry were not acceptable, since Dr. Hilton is at present not free to marry you. There are two options, either you return to Denmark or to Czechoslovakia and it is up to you to decide. We will then book you a flight and you will have to leave by this afternoon.' Sidney and I looked at each other, and felt as though the world around us had collapsed. We were so close to our dream to live together to come true, and now we would have to fight for it yet again. Also the decision seemed so senseless, for it was obvious that in the end I would be admitted to England and the delay just made it much more difficult for all of us, particularly for the children who would have to make two difficult adjustments instead of one.

I tried to explain this to the immigration officer, and he was, I think, sympathetic to my argument and slightly ill at ease but was unable to help us. 'I would rather return to Denmark, than to Czechoslovakia,' I said finally, and Sidney added, 'I will come with you and book a seat on the same flight.' He turned to the immigration officer and asked: 'Can I come with you to make the necessary arrangements?' Sidney gave me a hug, tried to look optimistic and said something like 'We will get there in the end,' before he left with the immigration officer. I was left alone with the children and felt desperate.

I put our things back into our little green suitcase, and needed an additional small bag for the toys Betty had brought for the children. When I was packed Sidney and an airline stewardess came and escorted us to board a British Airways flight for Copenhagen. The children were pleased to fly again, after all it was an exciting experience for them, but Sidney and I were in a sombre mood. We sat next to each other, took some comfort in touching each other as we held hands and waited for the plane to arrive to Copenhagen.

Back in Copenhagen.

On arrival the four of us—Sidney, myself and my two daughters —were taken into a room before passing through passport control. There a Danish immigration officer and a young very pretty blonde woman joined us. The young woman brought along some toys, and took the children into a quiet corner of the room, where she tried to entertain the children, while the officer asked me some questions: 'Dr. Vrbová, could you tell me about your Czechoslovak passport. Is it genuine or forged?' I told him that the passport was genuine, but that the addition of my childrens' names was carried out by me and was not authorized. He made a note of this and then asked: 'What do you want to do? Do you want to stay in Denmark, return to Czechoslovakia or live in Great Britain?' The answer was not difficult: 'I would like to settle in Great Britain, but I was not given permission to do so. As you can see the British immigration authorities have sent us back to Denmark. Could my children and I stay in Denmark until we are given a British visa?' The Danish officer smiled, and said: 'If this is what you want maybe we can work something out.' He looked at my passport and wrote down all the information on a piece of paper which he put into a folder. Then he asked Sidney a few questions about our relationship, and his intentions to marry me. He seemed to be satisfied with the information and summed up the discussion: 'Firstly, you do not want to return to Czechoslovakia; secondly, you do not want to stay permanently in Denmark, and thirdly, you want to be in Denmark transiently until you are granted a British visa. Is this correct?' When I agreed with this summary he smiled and started to fill in some papers. 'Well,' he said, 'I will try and help you to arrange this but I need my superiors to agree to this.' Having said this he left the room. Sidney and I sat huddled together and holding hands. I was exhausted and anxious.

The Danish immigration officer returned with a broad smile and said: 'It is all fixed, you can stay in Denmark as long as you want and for the immediate future we will try to help you to find accommodation for the children and yourself. Now we have to clarify a few details. I will have to take down all your personal details and file them. Then we will have to decide what sort of Danish identity papers we should issue for you. Again I will have to consult my colleague, for I do not want to make the decision alone.' He left the room and returned quickly. 'It is all sorted out,' he said, 'we will not issue you with any documents, because if we did so and you got a job you would have to pay taxes. Therefore it is best if officially you do not exist. I will give you a special telephone number in case you need to identify yourself to a bank if you open an account or to another organization.' He handed me an official paper with a number and said: 'You will ring this number and you will be asked the following question: who entered the names of your children into your passport? You will have to give the correct answer which of course is: myself. Then your identification will be confirmed.' I was a little bit taken aback, it was strange to suddenly cease to exist, but it was also fun. With these formalities completed, we were now admitted to Denmark and ushered through immigration control. I was handed a document informing the manager of a hostel to let us have a room for a few nights. A taxi was then summoned, all four of us settled in the car and the driver was then given an address of a hostel where recent immigrants were temporarily accommodated.

My daughters seemed to have had a good time at the airport; they got more presents and several new toys. Helena got a large doll with eyes almost as blue as hers and wonderful black eyelashes. She held the doll in her arm and cuddled it. Zuza had a *Donald Duck* with flexible legs and arms that Zuza could bend, which made her very happy. My present from the Danish immigration authorities was particularly generous: it was the permission to stay in Denmark for an unlimited time, which meant being together with Sidney or at least closer to him, for the time being. The immigration officer gave us the address of the hostel where we could stay temporarily. The taxi drove us to the hostel, a drab and shabby building in one of Copenhagen's less glamorous districts. We entered the lobby and found the receptionist, a plain elderly woman who was expecting us, since she had been already contacted by the immigration department. Fortunately she could speak a little English and Sidney tried to make the arrangements for us. She led the way up to the first floor, along a corridor lined with doors. She unlocked a door of a room that was nearly at one end of the corridor. It was a shabby room, with one double and two single beds. The furniture was dark brown, and the upholstery on the two easy chairs frayed. The paintwork was peeling, and the carpet was falling apart. It was a rather depressing place, and I knew that I would have to find something more cheerful. The woman explained that it was one of the better rooms with the advantage that the toilet and bathroom were close, just two doors away at the end of the corridor. Still for the next few days we would have to stay here. Sidney was even more upset with our accommodation than I, and we decided to turn to Morten yet again and ask for his help.

We left our suitcase in the room, and went to the reception to ask whether we could make a telephone call. We were directed to a cubicle in the reception area which had a 'phone and the receptionist put us through to an outside line. Sidney called Morten, described what had happened and told him that we were back in Denmark, needed to stay here for an uncertain time and were again in need of help. Morten promised to come and see us the next morning, and was confident that he could sort something out. We went out, found a small restaurant, had something to eat and returned to the hostel. All of us were exhausted and prepared to go to bed. The bathroom and toilet were at the end of the corridor, and before going to bed I took the children to the bathroom. The concrete floor of the corridor chilled our feet, and when we entered the bathroom and toilet I was taken aback by the grime and dirt. Still there was hot water and we could have a quick wash and dry ourselves with the threadbare towel provided. We went back to our room. Sidney could only stay with us for one night since he had to return to London to his work, but I was pleased that he was with us this first night in this horrible place. There was so much uncertainty that faced me about our future and I badly needed his reassurance and support.

Next morning Morten came, and Sidney handed us over to his care. After lengthy discussions two major decisions were taken: Morten would ask his parents whether the children and I could stay in their flat for a few weeks while they were in their summer house in Bornholm, a beautiful Island in the Baltic Sea. Morten thought that it would be possible for us to move in the following week. Also, I would try and get a job in Professor Buchthal's laboratory at the Institute of Neurophysiology.

Unfortunately and to my great disappointment Sidney had to return to London and go back to work. Before leaving Sidney called Professor Buchthal and arranged an appointment for me to see him. I was truly grateful to Sidney for his help, and happy that he proved to be such a loyal person.

When Sidney had left for the airport, Morten went to try and make arrangements for us to move to his parent's house and Helena, Zuza and I went to see Professor Buchthal at the Institute of Neurophysiology to investigate the possibility of my getting a job. Morten gave me excellent instructions as to how to find the place and I managed to follow them. The Institute was part of the University, and once we found the University campus we just followed the signposts to the Institute of Neurophysiology, and then to Professor Buchthal's office. I knocked on the door, and the three of us entered a large, spacious office. A handsome dark, middle aged man rose and greeted us. He pointed to some chairs and told us to be seated while he sat behind his desk. 'What can I do for you?' he asked, and added 'I know your work, and have great admiration for Ernest Gutmann. You come from a very interesting group. Sidney Hilton called me earlier and explained the circumstances that brought you to Denmark.' I was aware of the fact that landing in Professor Buchthal's office with two young children must have looked rather odd and not entirely professional, but then my situation was odd, and my visit was not entirely professional, but rather a cry for help to a colleague. I explained in broken English what had happened to me and why I had to stay in Denmark for a while until my problem with the British visa was resolved. 'I do not know how long I will be here, but I would like to spend my time doing something useful. I admire your work and would like to ask whether I could work in your Institute and learn from you some of the methods you pioneered.' The Professor looked me up and down, and then turned to the children. 'Do you like it here in Denmark?' He asked them in Danish. I was surprised, when Helena looked at him with her large blue eyes, smiled and answered in Danish 'Ja, tak (Yes, thank you)' for I didn't realize that my children had already picked up some Danish. I think this must have charmed Professor Buchthal, for he said that he would try and help us. 'I will introduce you to some of my colleagues and we will then try to find a project for you that would combine your existing experience with our interests. I will also try to find some money for you. Please come with me.' We left his office and went along the corridor to another office.

The room we entered was crowded with various electronic

equipment scattered on the desk, on the chairs and on the floor. The equipment almost obscured the tall lady sitting behind the desk and facing a large machine. Professor Buchthal introduced her, 'This is Anelise Rosenfalck, she will take care of you now, for I have to attend a meeting.' Then he talked with Anelise for a while in Danish, which I didn't understand and left. The children were fascinated by the equipment, with all those knobs and flashing lights. Anelise noticed their interest, smiled and said that she would show them what the big machine was for. She took two pairs of metal pads, covered them with gauze soaked in some liquid, presumably saline, told my daughters to bare their forearm and attached the pads to their forearm with a plaster. Then she switched on the machine and indicated to my children to move their hand. Both Helena and Zuza watched with fascination at what was happening. As they moved their wrist two of the six pens on the machine started to move at a great speed and when the children stopped moving their wrist the pens also stopped moving. 'We have just recorded the electrical activity your muscles produce when you move your joints. This is called electromyography, and this machine is one of the best ones to record this. Most of the work I do is to try and develop instruments that record electrical activity from muscles when they move.' This was a new toy for my children, but I could see that they had done enough of job hunting with me for one day and wanted to leave. We thanked Anelise, arranged to meet her the next day when she might have some more news about a possible job for me and left the Institute. I felt very grateful for having been given hope for a job.

We did some shopping for dinner and then made our way to the shabby hostel we were staying at. It was still light when we returned, and the more we examined our accommodation the worse it looked. There were other immigrants staying there and we met some of them in the corridor. Most of them were youngish, single men in their 20s. I had no idea where they came from, but somehow I was quite worried and felt that I could not let the children out of my sight and could not allow them to go to the bathroom on their own. After we had finished eating our dinner we went to bed, and I fell asleep. I was woken up in the middle of the night by Helena who crept into my bed and was rather alarmed. I was surprised, and asked what had happened. 'Maminko, I needed to go to the toilet and didn't want to wake you, so I took my doll with me and went on my own. On my way back to our room a man stopped me, got hold of my doll and asked me to come to his room to get it back. But I was frightened and ran to our room as fast as I could. I lost my doll.' I drew my daughter close to me, felt her soft body next to mine, stroked her dark hair and said, 'Helenka, you did the right thing to run to our room. We will get the doll back, but please do not go out on your own. I don't mind being woken up, if you need to go outside.' After that I checked that our door was locked. Helena stayed with me in my bed and soon fell asleep, but I was too distressed to sleep. We really had to get out of this place as fast as possible.

Morten came next morning and had good news for us. He told us that we could move into his parent's flat the same day. I packed our belongings and Morten took us to our next accommodation. Morten's father was an artist and the flat was full of landscape paintings. Most of them were of Bornholm, the small island in the Baltic Sea, where Morten's parents had a summerhouse. There were also many paintbrushes and paints scattered about, that Morten and

I collected and put on top of the cupboard so they should not get lost. Already the children kept asking whether they could use them. Morten offered to take care of Helena and Zuza, while I went to the Department of Neurophysiology to enquire about my job. Professor Buchthal was already waiting for me and gave me the good news that they would be able to employ me and pay me a small salary from a grant they had for a particular project. However, he said I would have to work on a project that he is interested in rather then choosing my own project. We then discussed the project, and agreed on how to proceed with the work. Although the project was of little interest to me, I was grateful to have been given a job, and appreciated Professor Buchthal's generosity in taking on someone he knew nothing about.

I met Anelise again, she smiled at me and gave me the good news that she had found a very good kindergarten near the Institute where my daughters could go to during the day. Anelise came with me to see the place straight away. I met Eva, the person in charge who showed me around and I was very impressed with both the facilities and the carers who worked there. I thought my daughters would like it too, and I made an appointment for them to come and see the kindergarten the next day.

When I returned to our 'new flat' and reported the news to Morten and the children I felt that our lives in Denmark would perhaps be better then I had expected.

Our year in Copenhagen.

The children settled in the kindergarten quite quickly and Helena acquired the affection of a boy called Toben. The two of them became inseparable. Both Helena and Zuza learned to speak Danish and could discuss their secrets in front of me, for I found Danish a very difficult language, and I still struggled with my English. In the Department everyone spoke English, and so I didn't feel the need to learn Danish.

I found it much more difficult to settle in Copenhagen than the children. I was desperately homesick and missed my friends and colleagues in Prague. I was also worried that they may be in trouble with the Secret Service (Statní Narodní Bezpečnost)) on account of my escape. To try and prevent this I wrote several letters to the Institute explaining that my escape was motivated only by personal and not political problems. The fear that was instilled in us in Czechoslovakia over the years also affected me during those early weeks in Denmark. Almost every night as soon as I fell asleep I dreamed that when I went to pick up my children from the kindergarten they wouldn't be there, and instead a stern Czech Secret Service man would meet me to tell me that they had taken Helena and Zuza to the Czechoslovak Embassy to be sent back to Prague. 'If you want to see them again you have to come with us.' So real seemed these events in my dream that I woke up drenched in sweat and rushed to check that the children were with me at home fast asleep. My health also took its toll and suffered from all the stress; I had mild fevers almost every evening. Each new person that entered Denmark had to undergo a routine health check. During my check up it was discovered that I had a small lesion in my left lung due to tuberculosis which fortunately had began to heal spontaneously. I was told to take it easy and rest, which of course I could not do.

With the onset of winter and cold weather we needed warm

clothes and I did not have enough money to buy them. In the mornings on our way to the kindergarten the dark streets were slippery with a splattering of snow and the leaden sky above us promised more snow or rain. 'Mummy, my feet and hands are cold,' Helena reminded me regularly, and she often cried because her feet and fingers hurt her. I was distressed that I could not provide her with basic needs, such as warm clothes for the winter.

I realized that I would have to get some warm things for my daughters and asked Eva the head of the kindergarten who was always very kind to us, for help. 'No problem,' she said, 'most families will be pleased to donate some used shoes and clothes to the kindergarten to make room for new things they will get for Christmas. I will see what we can do.' And so Eva fitted us out with warm shoes coats and trousers, but my daughters still had no smart dresses.

Christmas was approaching and we needed something smart for the parties organized by the kindergarten and my new friends and colleagues in the Department. I decided that I could sew some dresses from materials that I could purchase cheaply in the stores. I had no sewing machine so I sewed them by hand, and I thought my daughters looked very nice in these specially designed dresses.

And then we had a real windfall. One day I received a telephone call in the Department from a bank asking me to come along because they had some money for me. I went to the bank and was asked to identify myself. They took me to the manager, who was rather surprised that I had no documents to identify myself. Then I remembered the telephone number given to me by the immigration officer when we arrived back to Copenhagen, and called. They asked the agreed question:'Who put the names of your children into your passport?' When I gave the correct answer they confirmed my identity to the bank manager. When I was told that Sidney's father, whom I didn't even know, had sent us £800 as a Christmas present I was beside myself with joy! This seemed a real fortune to me, and it was a tremendous help. I went shopping to buy some Christmas presents for the children, and for some friends. Now that I had some money, the shops with their Christmas decorations and many luxury items displayed did not seem so forbidding any more. The Danes celebrate Christmas with a lot of light and decorations to dispel the dark short days and gloom typical of northern cities like Copenhagen.

Sidney came to visit and for the first time and we spent Christmas together as a family. It was a wonderful feeling and after all we did have a happy first Christmas in the West. I hoped that next year, 1959 would solve all our problems. Sidney would get his divorce and we would, at last, be able to live as a family in England. But I didn't anticipate that it would take another nine months.

The year 1959 started well for me. My work in the Department was more interesting than I expected and I learned many new things. Work started at 8 o'clock and each morning when all the members of the Department met and had coffee together. To my great surprise nobody talked during these gatherings, and I was told that this helped people to sort out their thoughts before starting work. On Mondays each member of staff had a meeting with Professor Buchthal to discuss their work and plan the next week's experiments. These meetings were important for we learned how to interpret our findings. Only later did I realize that I had the privilege to work in a Department that did pioneering work on the neuromuscular system that influenced a whole generation of neurologists and scientists. Also, I had made friends with some of the other members of staff and had developed a good social life.

In February 1959 things improved even more, for a Polish visitor, a young woman called Irena Hausmanowa-Petrusiewicz came to work in Professor Buchthal's department and we became very close, life-long friends. In fact our friendship continues to the present day. In those days in Copenhagen, when the days were short and Copenhagen was gloomy her friendship and support were like a glimpse of light. Gradually the winter lost its grip on the city, days became longer and spring arrived. Yet there still was no news about our visa to England, and I didn't know how long we would be stuck in Copenhagen.

Thanks to friends there were now several bright and exciting

Morten and his son and I in Bornholm.

episodes in our life. When Sidney came to visit in May, Morten took us to his parent's summerhouse in Bornholm. This small Island in the Baltic Sea is a real jewel, with green hills and clear streams where Morten caught trout barehanded. We went for long walks, the children roamed around the meadows, playing and enjoying the freedom.

Unfortunately when we returned to Copenhagen we had very sad news: Sidney's father, whom I had longed to meet, had suddenly died of a massive heart attack while we were in Bornholm. Sidney took the next plane and went to London, but both of us felt guilty that he wasn't with his father before he died.

Sidney's father and mother, Betty.

As spring progressed, preparation for the summer vacation were under way. In June, the kindergarten arranged to take all the children to the seaside for two weeks. The children explored the Baltic coast and learned about the plants and animals that inhabited it. On her return from this holiday Helena reported that this was the best holiday she had ever had. But this impression may have been coloured by the fact that her friendship with Toben flourished, and being able to spend a lot of time with him made the holiday for her especially enjoyable. I think Zuza felt terribly homesick and lonely, and didn't blend in with the other children as well as Helena. She also felt abandoned by Helenka's new relationship with Toben.

Helenka and Toben on their school holiday trip.

Our family holiday was planned for July when Sidney came to visit and his mother Betty, so recently widowed, decided to join us, so as to be with her son and us, his new family. We rented a flat near Tilsted in Jutland near a fjord and spent a wonderful three weeks swimming, walking and tasting all sorts of seafood. The weather was kind to us and most days Betty packed our swimming things, made sandwiches and we set out to explore the coast. Sidney and I basked in the sun lying in the soft sand. I enjoyed watching Betty's athletic figure in her black elegant swimming costume wading into the water, holding the hands of my daughters and encouraging them to venture into the cold North Sea. In the shallow water near the beach Helena swam on her own, but Zuza had to be supported by a rubber ring, or by 'grandmother' Betty holding her by putting her hand under her tummy and instructing her to make the right movements with her arms and legs to propel herself forward. Then one day Betty let go of Zuza and Zuza managed to swim on her own. Betty was delighted and proud that she had taught Zuza to swim. It was during this holiday that I became very fond of Betty, and appreciated her affection for my children, and her acceptance of her son's unorthodox relationship with this stranger that was me. Our holiday ended and we returned to Copenhagen. Betty departed back to London and Sidney stayed with us for a few more days.

On our return a letter from Sidney's solicitors was waiting for him. It contained the good news that Sidney's divorce was almost complete and that he would be getting his *decree nisi* within the next few weeks. When Sidney told me this he took me in his arms and held me close. 'We can marry now,' he said, 'and I want you to come to London as soon as I can arrange with the Home Office that they will allow you to enter England, now that I am free to marry you.' I was excited about this, but didn't quite believe it. Moreover there were many arrangements I had to make in Copenhagen before setting off for England, and leaving my new friends saddened me. But I was filled with joy that at last Sidney and I would be starting our life together. 'Now that we know that we will soon be setting up our own home, let's go shopping and buy some things for our future home,' Sidney suggested. So we bought a beautiful Danish cutlery set and several other things. It was a wonderful feeling to be setting up our future home at last.

Sidney went back to London, and then eventually at the end of September, I received the news that my visa had been granted provided I marry Sidney within one month after entering England. I didn't like the idea of being forced to marry anyone, but since this agreed with my own wishes, I didn't object.

Sidney came to Copenhagen to help us to pack up our things. I was delighted for I felt now we were moving as a family. We had too much luggage to take with us on a plane and decided to take the boat from Esjberg to Harwich and arrive to England by sea. Unlike when leaving Prague, here we could express a real goodbye to all our friends, for no secret police force was watching over us. It was at this stage that I realized how many new attachements all three of us had formed during the time we stayed in Copenhagen.

Chapter 15
Starting Life In England

Sidney and I, London 1959.

Arrival and wedding.

On a grey and wet morning on the 1st October 1959, more than one year after we had left Czechoslovakia, our boat from Denmark carrying Sidney, Helena, Zuza and I docked at Harwich. We desembarked, and lined up to have our passport checked. Although my Danish passport for homeless people that we obtained in Copenhagen before our departure, had a British visa valid for one month, I still couldn't believe that this time we will be allowed to enter this unwelcoming country. The reason given for granting me a visa to visit Britain was 'marriage', and I had to get married within one month. My visa in the Danish passport seemed to have satisfied the immigration officer in Harwich so that this time there was no problem with the immigration authorities and we were allowed onto British soil. We collected our luggage and headed for the exit. Before sailing to pick us up from Denmark Sidney left his car parked in Harwich, and the four of us headed towards the car park where Sidney pointed out his small, pale blue Austin Mini. I had never owned a car, and to me the little Mini seemed a real luxury. We and the luggage squeezed into the car and Sidney told me that we would drive straight to his mother's flat and stay there for a few days. Apparently all was arranged for our wedding which was planned to take place in a week's time. We were leaving Harwich driving on a road leading to London and to the beginning of our new life. I felt that our family life in our new home had started, and that our problems were over.

Nevertheless, in spite of my joy and happiness that at last Sidney and I were together I was apprehensive about our future. Sadness and nostalgia filled me, as I thought about my past life in Prague, the friends and colleagues that cared about me and the children, the affection and love we had for each other. I had left behind all that and I had little knowledge what our lives would be like here in this cold, wet and grey country. I tried to convince myself that life for all of us would be better here in this country, which I would like to adopt to become my home, and I was determined to confront many unknown obstacles. However, the immediate task was our wedding, and finding some accommodation where we could live together.

After what seemed to me an endless drive, Sidney stopped the car in front of his mother's flat in Onslough Gardens in Knightsbridge, behind Harrods. Betty, my future mother-in-law, whom we already knew and liked very much, was waiting for us in her luxurious flat. While we were in Denmark, her husband had died of a sudden heart attack and she was still suffering from this loss. Nevertheless, she prepared a very generous welcome for us. She had some toys ready for my daughters and I was grateful to her for remembering them and trying to give them a treat to welcome them to their new country. Betty was very smartly dressed in a grey woollen fitted dress and blended well into the luxurious surroundings both outside and inside her flat. She had lunch prepared for us: melon as an hors d'oeuvre and followed by fresh salmon which I tasted for the first time in my life. While having lunch we discussed the arrangements for our wedding and our accommodation. The wedding was scheduled to take place in a few days time at Kensington Town Hall, and a reception in Betty's flat was to follow, where I would meet and be introduced to Sidney's family members and some friends. The problem was I had no smart dress that would be suitable for the occasion. When I voiced my concern, Betty suggested that I could wear one of her dresses. We were of similar size and I could choose which dress I would like. I was too overcome with new impressions and apprehensive of what the future had in store for us, to worry too much about what to wear. After all, the wedding was just a necessary formality.

Next morning Betty drove us in her car to the temporary accommodation she had found for us. It was a two-roomed furnished flat with a bathroom and small kitchen in the first floor of a house in Woodstock Road, Golders Green, North London, which a Jewish family, called Wosner, rented out. The flat was rather shabby and unfriendly, but the landlords, the

Wosners, were a nice couple that seemed to be pleased to have children in the flat. They had a television, which for us was a novelty, and they offered that the children could come to their sitting room and watch the television whenever they wanted.

The next few days went by very fast. I was eager to find a school for my daughters and we went to visit the school nearest to our flat, which was Wessex Gardens school. It seemed to me to be a friendly place, the Head Teacher was welcoming, and promised to make sure that my daughters would get help to learn English fast and will be helped to become integrated in their class. Helena was very positive, and keen to start. It was now the beginning of October and all the children of her age had already been at school for three weeks. Zuza however was not so keen. She felt that after having adjusted once to a Danish kindergarten, it was too much to change again to a school where she did not know anyone, and could not communicate. I felt very sorry for her, for it was really hard for her to have to adjust yet again to so many new things.

Our wedding took place in the morning of the 6th October 1959 in Kensington Town Hall. I wore my mother-in-law's 'little black dress' which was completely out of place for the occasion, but it was the only one I liked, from Betty's elaborate wardrobe. It was the most unromantic wedding imaginable, and I felt really gloomy, and not ready to face a reception. After the 'ceremony' we returned to Betty's flat for lunch and later for a party with Sidney's family. Betty had arranged the catering and to me it seemed lavish. I had never seen so many exotic snacks and canopies before and such a selection of various drinks. Even more strange and alien were members of Sidney's family. Most of them were dressed in rather expensive clothes and looked at the children and me as though we were strange specimens imported to their family. They complained to Betty and Sidney that we didn't have a wedding at the synagogue and since we didn't speak much English ignored me and the children. Most members of Sidney's family were affluent middle class Jewish business men or professionals such as lawyers or doctors. Their conversation concentrated around news as to who had done well in their profession, how much money they earned and about people I didn't know. Most conspicuous and memorable was the wife of Betty's brother, Aunt Rose, a corpulent lady who was a staunch supporter of the conservative party, with no compassion or sympathy for people less fortunate than her. I was stunned by this assembly, so different from my own family I remembered from home, where a newcomer would have been made to feel welcome and where everyone would have liked to have learned more about new members of the family. I was struck by this indifference and very cold reception we got from Sidney's family, particularly since Betty was such a wonderful warm person who was giving us so much love and support. She made up for all the disappointing members of the family, worked hard to make us feel welcome, and I appreciated her effort and generosity. When the guests left we packed our things, and next day Sidney the children and I moved to our flat in Golders Green in North London.

Settling down.

The first morning in our new flat Sidney and I took Helena and Zuza to their new school, in Wessex Gardens hoping they will settle well. They were taken to their respective classes and I was told to pick them up at 3:30 in the afternoon. Each day between 8:30 am and 3:30 pm I was free to look for a job. Sidney was trying to help me and a friend of his who was Professor of Pharmacology at the Royal Free Hospital Medical School offered to interview me with the possibility of offering me a position of a Research Assistant. This was good news and I couldn't wait to go to meet her. The Department was then in Huntley Street, near King's Cross station, in easy reach from Golders Green. I took the Northern line on the underground, exited at King's Cross station and walked along Euston Road, until I found Huntley Street and the Department of Pharmacology. I knocked at the door of Sidney's friend who was Professor of Pharmacology. When I entered I was greeted by a very attractive, well groomed red-haired lady who introduced herself as Nora Zaimis and told me that she too is an immigrant and comes from Greece. After a short interview she gave me the good news and said that I could start work as a Research Assistant as soon as I wanted. She introduced me to the other members of the Department and I was delighted to have my first job in England.

There still was a lot to do before I could start work; I had to arrange to get British citizenship now that I was legally married to an Englishman, help the children to get settled in their new school and try to get to know some of Sidney's friends. Sidney and I enjoyed our new life and it seemed to be wonderful to be at last 'permanently' together. Sidney was keen to make me feel part of his life and meet his friends and colleagues. My English improved rapidly and I had little difficulty taking part in conversations or discussions. Although we were often invited to join Sidney's friends for dinner we seldom went out, for then we would have had to leave the children at home and get a babysitter. This was difficult because of the language barrier and I did not want to leave the children with someone they could not communicate with. It was not a habit here to invite children as well as their parents. Only one single time were we invited out as a family with both my daughters. It was Sidney's colleague Vivian Abrahams who invited all four of us for tea to his house in Harrow. It was some time before Christmas, a sunny Sunday afternoon when the four of us drove to Vivien's house. The children were made to feel welcome, and Vivien and his wife Pam took part in various games we played together with Helena and Zuza. We had tea, with sandwiches followed by scones, stawberry jam and cream. This was one of those occasions when I felt that maybe, I could get used to this place. Meanwhile, Sidney and I were looking for a house to buy together where we would settle and have more space for Helena and Zuza. Sidney and I wanted children and we needed a proper home. We could only afford a small mortgage, for reasons I didn't understand, since Sidney's family was really rich and where I came from this usually was shared. First we looked at houses in a district called Hampstead Garden Suburb, but these were too expensive, and for some reason Sidney wanted to move west, so we ended up in Kenton, in the heart of London's suburbia.

Suburbia.

Our house was very attractive. It was a four bedroom semi-detached house, solidly built in the 1930s. It had leaded windows, a garden and a very good primary school just across the street. It was in a quiet, leafy street and close to the underground station. Sidney and I liked it a lot, and were happy when we moved in. Moving was not difficult, for we had hardly any furniture. Sidney had an uncle in Leeds who had a furniture store and very generously supplied us with two single beds, one double bed a dining room table and four chairs. We had to pay very little for all this for he gave us a large discount. Betty gave us many kitchen utensils and since the house had a fitted kitchen we were all set to be independent. This was a very good start for us. We moved in late spring and when the children's school finished in summer we enjoyed the garden. This was the first time that I had a garden and it gave me great pleasure. We bought a paddling pool and a climbing frame for the children. Strangely though, it was through this novelty of having my very own garden that I first experienced the peculiar attitude of English people to the human body. Back home in Czechoslovakia and also in Denmark children could sunbathe or paddle naked, particularly in their own home, and so I allowed Helena and Zuza to run around our private garden without wearing any clothes. To my astonishment, my neighbour knocked at the door. I opened the door and asked her in, but she refused to enter the house and in an angry voice told me that she found it offensive that the children were in the garden without any clothes. I was astonished, and found this intrusion into our privacy particularly offensive. I thought only in the Eastern Bloc countries was spying on ones' neighbours acceptable. There the spying was about political opinions, here about how I treated my children.

After six months at the Royal Free Hospital my grant expired and I had to look for new employment. I wanted to continue the work I was involved in while I was in Prague, and it so happened that a colleague, Dr Arthur Buller, who was a lecturer at the Physiology Department at Kings College had similar interests. I went to Kings

College in the Strand to see him, discussed my work with him and asked him whether he could give me space for a small laboratory where I could work supported by a grant from the Medical Research Council (MRC) which I was promised. Arthur was quite positive, and asked me to come and see him in a few days time. We arranged to meet at Kings College and have lunch together. I arrived at Arthur's office, said 'Hello,' and commented that he was wearing a very attractive tie. He gave me a most surprising and unexpected answer, 'An English woman would never make such a personal comment to a man she hardly knows.' Well, I obviously did not behave like an English woman, and found it difficult to understand why my colleague objected to my comment about his tie, after all a tie is not a very personal item. Then we went for lunch to a small café in the Strand. While discussing various problems related to my possible work at Kings College, Arthur looked at my hand and said: 'When you first came I noticed that you had a wedding ring on your finger, and today you are not wearing one. Are you married?' I had no idea why I was asked this question, it had nothing to do with work, or anything else related to my job. Still I was in no position to argue so I told the truth: 'I was cleaning the house we just moved into and removed my wedding ring. I am married to Sidney Hilton, even though I am not wearing my ring today.' This answer seemed to have satisfied Arthur and he offered me space in his group at Kings College. I got the promised grant from the MRC and this gave me an excellent start to build up my own research project.

Yet a particular aspect of my new situation baffled me and this concerned the attitudes of my English male colleagues and Institutions towards women. Incomprehensible to me was the fact that women were not allowed to use the common room at Kings College, and I always wondered what went on in this room to make it necessary to exclude women. But the 60s were just around the corner—heralding the decade for feminism—and it was a most welcome movement that would secure the British women the rights and position women in Eastern Europe enjoyed. Within a reasonably short time the attitude towards women in the UK changed, though it took decades to approach the degree of freedom that I experienced as a career woman in Czechoslovakia.

Everyday life was so much easier for me now: there were shops where food was readily available and shopping was a pleasure. Items that we did not even dream of in Czechoslovakia such as oranges or bananas were easy to buy and the selection of clothes and other consumables was enormous. No more queueing for potatoes or meat like back in Czechoslovakia. We could also travel freely wherever we wanted to, and had the freedom to complain about the government or anything else. Yet there were other types of freedom that I missed in my new country and these concerned the attitudes of my English male colleagues and Institutions to women. Nevertheless, I was exuberant and happy with my new existence, I had a job that was interesting and a bright future to look forward to.

Helena with baby Caroline, 1964.

Epilogue

My daughter Zuza Vrbová, London 1972.

After I left Czechoslovakia and my one year interlude in Denmark I have spent most of my life in England. My husband Sidney and I spent 12 years together and while we were married we had two lovely children, Caroline and Peter. We started our life in London, and in spite of many prejudices against women and foreigners I managed to continue my work. I was fortunate, for Sidney helped me to understand how the British scientific establishment worked and instructed me how to write papers and grant applications.

In 1964 Sidney became Chairman of the Department of Physiology at the University of Birmingham and we moved to Birmingham. I too had a position in the Department of Physiology. At the time I was distressed about the move, for it meant that my two older daughters, Helena and Zuza, had to endure yet another change. We found a house close to the University, so that the move to Birmingham had some compensation for I could spend more time with the children at home. My work in Birmingham was very enjoyable. I supervised several PhD students, and our research became recognized.

However, the emotional stresses of our efforts to accommodate conflicting interests into a happy family life began to manifest themselves. I brushed under the carpet signs of Sidney's failure to cope with a new job as well as participating in family life. I was therefore taken by surprise when Sidney returned from a research visit to Sweden and told me that he no longer wanted to live with me and the family. I tried to keep the family together. Helena was a medical student at Edinburgh University, Zuza was completing her A-levels and Caroline and Peter were still very young, and needed a father. I really did not want to be a single parent. To give us time to sort things out, and think how to mend the cracks in our relationship, I went for a sabbatical to Melbourne in Australia with Zuza, Caroline and Peter. (Helena did not want to interrupt her medical studies). It was in Australia that I realized that to remedy my relationship with Sidney was probably hopeless. This was brought home to me when Sidney sent me a letter that revealed his real feelings towards me:

'I have to write to you about a sticky matter. I feel that whatever we decide about our future it would be most unwise for you to be working much longer in this Department.' I was deeply hurt, by being 'sacked' by my husband, and by being treated in a most unprofessional manner. But the final straw was the realization that not only did Sidney not care about me, he did not care about Helena, Zuza and his own children.

In spite of being disillusioned with Sidney, I still wanted to give our marriage a chance, but he decided to leave us, divorce and marry his secretary. Both Caroline and Peter have made a good life for themselves and have lovely children. Unfortunately, Sidney has never seen his grandchildren. Falling in love with Sidney was a great mistake, but I don't regret it, for having Caroline, Peter and their children compensates for all the pain and disappointment inflicted by Sidney.

After our divorce I took a prestigious job at University College, London.. On a sunny day, in May 1976 I drove to London with my daughter Caroline find an area we would like to live in. I had a cousin who lived in Muswell Hill, and we had a look at the area. We drove through Cranley Gardens, a street lined with trees covered in cherry blossom and the sight took my breath away. We bought a house in this area of North London with a wonderful view across London all the way to the Kent downs. My children grew up and left to start their own families, and I am still here, enjoying the view and the very much improved London. In spite of the Iron Curtain I managed to keep in touch and meet my friends, with whom I shared so much while living in Czechoslovakia, quite often. While it was impossible for me to go to Czechoslovakia until 1989 my friend Hanka and I regularly met in Budapest. Indeed, at one of these meetings I smuggled a Sinclair computer to Hungary, for her to take back to Prague for her son. After the *Velvet Revolution* Czechoslovakia reverted to becoming a free and democratic country, and I am still rediscovering my homeland during my visits. Sadly, many of my friends are no longer there.

Looking back at my life I recognize that whether in socialist Czechoslovakia or capitalist England I was not much good at choosing suitable partners, or making the relationship work and I am sorry that my children had to suffer the consequences of this. Reading through the pages of this manuscript I realize that I am presenting the life in communist Czechoslovakia in rather rosy colours. Yet my description of our life under communism is accurate. I have not dwelt on the miscarriages of justice of the Communist Regime towards a large number of people, neither have I described the regrettable suffering of many of my friends and colleagues who had to struggle to earn a decent living and suffered a number of deprivations only because they voiced their disapproval of the system, or were otherwise victimized for being Jewish, middle class et cetera. Perhaps the reasons for not having been more outraged at these injustices are to be found in my past, where nothing done by the Czechoslovak post war totalitarian system could be compared to my experiences during the Holocaust. After all, we were allowed to live, and that to me seemed a real gift. I realize that this explanation does not make the cruelties and trespasses of humanitarian principles acceptable, but our generation was tarnished by experiences so terrible that our standards were different from what they should have been and what they are today. I would therefore like the reader of these pages to be aware that in the context of the post war period and my experiences during the war the reality of the communist system appeared different from what it seems to be looking back at it now. It is also possible that the distorted attitudes towards moral issues our generation acquired during the war and Nazi rule helped the Communist Regime to perpetrate atrocities that in a different time and looked at from a different perspective would have been unacceptable to the population. It perhaps answers the questions often asked by my children and grandchildren: 'How could you live under communism and not do anything to oppose the regime?' It was in part lack of courage, but not entirely, for to us the yardstick of human values was forged during Nazi rule, and communism in Czechoslovakia was incomparably better then what we had to endure before.

My experiences in England in the late 1950s and 1960s also taught me that there are many kinds of freedom. In those days a working mother, and perhaps a factory worker had many more advantages in communist Czechoslovakia that he or she would have had in democratic Britain. Although in Czechoslovakia we lacked freedom of expression there was good provision for young children and a long maternity leave. Also there was no prejudice against women at work. The trade unions in communist Czechoslovakia, made sure that workers had easy access to holidays, and cultural events such as theatre and music. Tickets were cheap, easily affordable and sold at the workplace. In England these privileges were restricted to those who could afford them.

Nevertheless, the fact that in a democracy one is in charge of one's own life is a tremendous gift, and nothing can compensate for it. I am very lucky that I have spent most of my life in Great Britain.

Caroline and Peter Hilton, my two youngest children, and I, Birmingham 1970.

Memorial for my parents, Trnava Jewish Cemetry 2006: *From left to right*: Andrew Jackson, (Zuza's husband), Pavol, Zuza, Me, Katka, Rudolf Klein and Karol Sidon.

My family—children and grandchildren—celebrating the launch of my book, ***Trust and Deceit*** in 2006**.**

From left to right first row: Hannah, Jack, Caroline, Zoe, Me, Zuza, Danny, Andrew; *second row:* Tim, Jane, Matthew, Peter, Jan.

LIST OF PARTICIPANTS

Abrahams Vivian and Pam Ch.15, Vivian became Head of the Department of Physiology at Kingston Ontario, Canada and moved to Canada. He and family are still there.
Ada Frank Ch. 3, 10. Died in Budapest of lung cancer in 1965.
Arthur Frank Ch. 3, 10. Died in Budapest 1982.
Andor Greiner Ch. 3, 10. Died in Budapest 1988.
Arnold Frank Ch. 5. Emigrated to Israel. Died in 1978.

Beneš Eduard Ch. 7. Second President of Czechoslovakia. Died 1948.
Beránek Radan Ch. 5, 9, 13. Member of the scientific team at the Institute of Physiology, Czechoslovak Academy of Science, Prague. Died in 1968.
Brodski Z Ch. 8. Obstetrician.
Buchthal F. Ch. 14. Clinical Neurophysiologist in Copenhagen. Died in the USA .
Buller A. Ch.15. Physiologist. Whereabouts unknown to me.
Burešová Olga Ch. 10. Staff member of the Institute of Physiology of the Czechoslovak Academy of Science. Died in 2008.

Chytil Franta Ch.9. Biochemist in Czechoslovakia. Whereabouts unknown to me.

Dvořáčková (Tetinka) Ch.8. 9, 10, 11, 12, 13. Childrens Nanny. Lived in Prague. Her fate after 1958 is unknown to me.
Dreyfus Jean Ch.9. French biochemist. Died.
Ďus Ch. 4 Julius Sidon, lives in Los Angeles, USA.

Eliana Ch.3. Czech scientist. Fate unknown to me.
Elszka Ch.13. Elszbieta Jankowska, Polish neurophysiologist. Lives in Göteborg, Sweden.
Ervin Stark Ch. 10. Hungarian scientist. Founding member of the Institute of Experimental Medicine, Budapest. Died from intraspinal tumour 1978.
Eva Ch. 1. Pediatrician, lives in Prague and USA.
Eva from Copenhagen Ch.14, Kindergarten teacher. Lived in Copenhagen. Present whereabouts unknown to me.

Fábry Pavel Ch. 11. Czech doctor and scientist. Died in 1980.
Fanči Ch. 4. Rudi's stepsister. Lived in Pieštany, Czechoslovakia died 2001.
Field Noel Ch.7. American accused of being a secret agent by the communist

Hungarian and Czech governments in the late 1940s.
Friedman Rose Ch.15. Wife of my mother-in-law's brother.

Gerber Imre Ch.10. Husband of my relative Baby. Emigrated from Hungary to the USA and died there.
Gerber children. Ch. 3, 10. Naomi (Mayo), Daisy and Bencze. Emigrated from Hungary to the USA. Live in California.
Gomułka Władislav, Ch.10. Became Head of Government in Poland in 1956 and introduced a less repressive administration. Died in 1982.
Gotwald Klement Ch. 7. Was President of Czechoslovakia. Died in 1952.
Gregorová Inge Ch. 1, 2, 3, 4. Retired biochemist, lived in Prague, Czech Republic. Died 2010.
Gregor Bubo Ch 3. Retired chemist. Lives in Prague.
Gutmann E. Ch .5, 9, 10, 11, 12. Distinguished scientist. Lived in Prague. Died prematurely in 1975.

Hausmanowa-Petrusiewicz Irena. Ch.14. Polish neurologist. Lives in Warsaw Poland.
Helena Vrbová. Dedication. Ch. 8, 9, 10, 11, 12, 13, 14, 15. Rudi's and Gerta's daughter. Medical doctor. Studied tropical diseases. Died in 1982.
Hilton Sidney, Ch. 9,10, 11,12, 13, 14, 15. Former husband of Gerta. Retired physiologist, lives in Wales.
Hilton Beth: Ch 9. Former wife of Sidney Hilton, died 2005.
Hilton Betty: Ch. 14, 15. Mother of Sidney Hilton. Lived in London then Brighton. Died 1985.
Hník Pavel: Ch.5. Member of staff of the Institute of Physiology, Czechoslovak Academy of Science. Died 2008.
Hudlická Olga Ch. 8 , 9. Member of staff of the Institute of Physiology of the Czechoslovak Academy of Science. Emigrated to England, and now lives in Birmingham, UK.

Ilonka Reichsfeldová Ch. 1,2, 3, 4. Mother of Rudi Vrba. Lived in Bratislava with her husband. Died in 1995.

Kamenický Anton Ch. 3, 4. Worked at the Foreign Office of the Czechoslovak Government. Died in 1995.
Karoušková Hanka. Ch. 9, 10, 11, 12. Retired employee of the Institute of

Physiology of the Czechoslovak Academy of Science. Lives in Prague, Czech Republic.
Karoušek Jakub. Ch.9. Lives in Prague, Czech Republic.
Kostyuk Platon. Ch.13. Neurophysiologist in Kiyev, Ukraine.
Křeček Z. Ch. 4. Retired employee of the Institute of Physiology of the Czechoslovak Academy of Science. Lives in Prague.
Krejčová Anna. Ch. 9. Retired employee of the Institute of Physiology of the Czechoslovak Academy of Sciences.

Laporte Yves. Ch.9. French neurophysiologist. Lives in France
Lysenko. Ch.7. Russian geneticist. Favoured by Stalin.
Little Olga. Ch.8. lives in London.

Manci Greiner. Ch. 3, 10. My Aunt. Lived in Budapest. Died 1988.
Maria. Ch. 3. Whereabouts unknown.
Marushka. Ch.1. Whereabouts unknown.
Minárik Laco. Ch. 4. Physician, has lived in Slovakia and Canada.
Mordowicz Czeszlaw. Ch. 3, 4. Friend of Rudi Vrba. Lived in Slovakia. Died in Toronto, Canada in 2000.
Morten Simonsen Ch.14. Danish immunologist and close friend of Sidney Hilton and Gerta. Died in Copenhagen in 2007.

Novotný Antonin. Ch.10. President of Czechoslovakia 1957-1968. Died in 1978.

Pavelka Ch.1. Friend of family. Whereabouts unknown.
Pavlov I.P. Ch. 7. Russian physiologist and psychologist, 1849—1936. Received Nobel Prize in 1904.
Pendimanz Pani. Ch.12. Polish peasant in Zakopané.
Purkrábek Ch.3. Technician in the Department of Anatomy, Charles University Prague. Whereabouts unknown.

Rosen Ch. 3, 4. Friend of Rudi Vrba. Wherabouts unknown.
Rosenfalk Aneli.se Ch.14. Staff member of the Institute of Neurophysiology, University of Copenhagen. Wherabouts unknown.
Rychlik Ivan Ch.5. Member of the Institute of Chemistry of the Czechoslovak Academy of Science. Whereabouts unknown.

Šling Otto. Ch. 7. Member of Czechoslovak Parliament and Communist Party. Accused of treason and executed during the Slánský trials in 1952. Rehabilitated in 1963.
Servit Zdeněk. Ch. 5. First Chairman of the Institute of Physiology of the Czechoslovak Academy of Sciences 1954. Died in 1986.
Sergey. Ch. 1. Russian Officer. Whereabouts unknown.
Šimončič Ch. 1. Whereabouts unknown.
Šik Otta. Ch.3. Czech medical student in 1945—1950.

Slánský Rudolf Ch.7. General Secretary of the Czechoslovak Communist Party after the Second World War. Accused of treason and executed in 1952.
Stalin Josef .Ch.7. Head of the Soviet Union. Died 1956
Svoboda Ch.8. Solicitor in Prague. Whereabouts unknown.

Toben Ch.14. Whereabouts unknown.

Ungar Alfred. Ch.1.Husband of my cousin Margareth. Lived in Vienna. Died 1970.

Voda Pavel. Ch. 9. Employee of the Czechoslovak Secret Service.
Vrba Rudi. Ch. 1, 2, 3, 4, 5, 6, 7, 8 ,9, 10. Gerta's first husband. Lived in London, UK and then Vancouver, Canada. Died in 2008.

Wetzler Freddie. Ch. 2, 3, 4. Friend of Rudi Vrba. Lived in Bratislava. Died 1988.

Zaimis Eleanor. Ch. 15. Head of Department of Pharmacology at the Royal Free Hospital, Medical School, London. Died in 1982.
Zelená J. Ch. 9. Czech scientist. Lives in Karlovy Vary.
Zbrożyna Andrzej. Ch. 13. Polish neurophysiologist. Moved to England and lives in Birmingham, UK.
Zbrożyna Barbara Ch.13. Polish sculptress. Died 1995.
Zbrożyna Jacek Ch.13. Brother of Andrzej. Whereabouts unknown.
Zigmond. Ch. 3. Polish medical student. Whereabouts unknown.
Zuza Ch. 8, 9, 10, 11, 12, 13, 14, 15. Gerta and Rudi's daughter. Writer of childrens' books. Lives in Cambridge, UK.

An earlier autobiographical title by Gerta Vrbová: ***Trust and Deceit***
A Tale of Survival in Slovakia and Hungary, 1939—1945.
(published by Vallentine Mitchell 2006; isbn 0 85303 630 6).

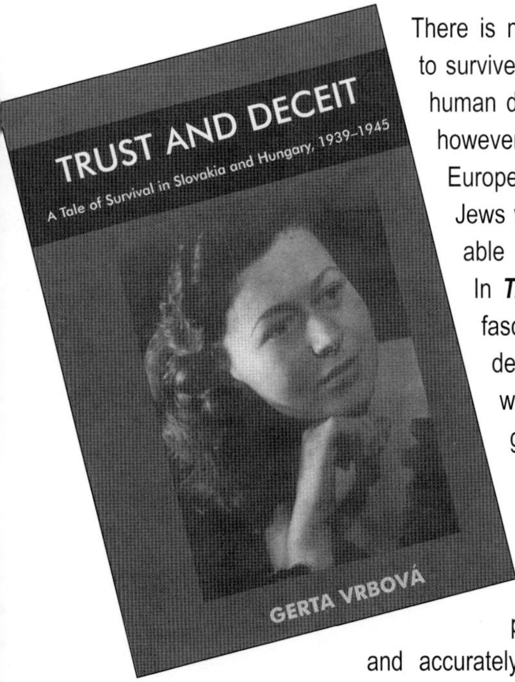

There is nothing biologically more important than to survive life-threatening situations without losing human dignity. History is full of tragic examples, however, none on such a scale as the Holocaust in Europe in the last century. There were not many Jews who survived it and still fewer who were able to give an accurate personal account. In ***Trust and Deceit*** the author reveals the fascinating psychology of a teenage girl dealing with the immense cruelties of the world. The book inspires the search for how genocide could be prevented in the future, and the truly heroic story will inspire anyone to survive—against all odds.

Trust and Deceit is a true and thrilling personal account of our modern history and accurately depicts the social and demographic structure of European society during the Holocaust years. The moral distortions of a society that made these surreal events possible to unfold are completely breathtaking.

About the Author:
Gerta Vrbová, lived through the Holocaust as an adolescent girl, in Nazi-occupied Slovakia and Hungary. Her lust for life, inborn gifts to adapt to special situations and react decisively, enabled her to survive. After the war, Gerta studied Medicine at Charles University in Prague in communist Czechoslovakia, and went on to become recognized in the field of Neuroscience. She lives in North London and her children and grandchildren live nearby.